Democracy, Eh?
A Guide to Voter Action

Canadian Cataloguing in Publication Data
Deverell, John, 1944-

Democracy, Eh! : a guide to voter action

ISBN 1-895854-15-6

1. Representative government and representation - Canada.   2.
Elections - Canada   3. Democracy - Canada.   4. Campaign - Ca-
nada.   5. Radio in politics - Canada.   6. Television in politics -
Canada.   I. Vézina, Greg, 1957-   .   II. Title.

JL167.D48 1993   324.6'3'0971   C93-097221-X

*We would be pleased to keep you on our mailing list for new
catalogues. Please send your name and address to :*

**Robert Davies Publishing, P.O. Box 702,
Outremont, QC H2V 4N6**

John Deverell & Greg Vezina

Democracy, Eh?
A Guide to Voter Action

ROBERT DAVIES PUBLISHING
MONTREAL–TORONTO

DISTRIBUTED IN CANADA BY

Stewart House
481 University Avenue, Suite 900
Toronto, Ontario M5G 2E9

☎ (Ontario & Quebec) 1-800-268-5707
☎ (rest of Canada) 1-800-268-5742

*To Brian Mulroney, Bob Rae and all the other
first ministers who made us wonder why,
in a country that calls itself a democracy,
politicians with so little public support
have so much power.*

TABLE OF CONTENTS

Chapter Four / The Politics of Inclusion: Citizen Lawmaking 101

Chapter Five / Open Democratic Government 132

Chapter Six / Teledemocracy: Opening the Channels 153

PREFACE
AND ACKNOWLEDGMENTS

THE DEMOCRACY, EH? project became a possibility in May 1990, the day *The Toronto Star* sent Deverell, a middle-aged, leftish, cynical political reporter to cover an unlikely event — the prosecution of the CBC, CTV and Global television networks by Citizen Vezina, frustrated inventor, Tory reformer and legal strategist for the Green Party of Canada.

Memories of the authors' first encounter are now obscured by time but Deverell's view, roughly, was that being right about illegal political broadcasting by the networks would do Vezina no good: the judicial system would chew him up, spit him out, and bankrupt him for good measure. Vezina's view was that the corruption of democracy had to be challenged and if nobody else in Canada would do it, he personally would find a way.

The court cases dragged on, and each time a judge gave an unfavorable ruling Vezina raged and the reporter shrugged. Finally this spring, with a federal election coming and neither of us able to find anyone in our acquaintance with positive voting intentions, the moment of decision came. "There's got to be a book," said Vezina, staring balefully at the reporter. Deverell, knowing there was a largely unpublicized four-volume report by the Royal Commission on Electoral Reform and Party Financing on hand, complete with 22 volumes of background research, agreed there had to be a book in it all somewhere — provided that the writing of it didn't make either of our bank managers more nervous than they were already.

An angel, chairman Frank Stronach of Magna International Corp., appeared. Stronach has strong, well-developed opinions on the failings of Canadian democracy and the party political system, but he put up generous financial assistance without trying to predetermine the shape or direction of our inquiry. For that liberating act of democratic faith and generosity we will always be grateful. Robert G. Brooks provided additional financial support, and The Toronto Star unhesitatingly allowed Deverell a leave of absence to pursue the project.

Several people provided assistance during the research and writing period: MP Dennis Mills lent steady encouragement and his staff, especially Diane Scharf in Ottawa and Bob Singleton in Toronto, were helpful in a dozen ways; Gordon Cressy introduced Deverell to the friendly and patient staff of the University of Toronto's Robarts Library; Leah McInnes of the Donner Canadian Foundation made its electoral reform research papers available to us; and BC MLA Ujjal Dosanjh, Chairman of the BC Select Standing Committee on Parliamentary Reform and Ethical Conduct, authorized his researchers to share with us the committee's materials on the citizen Initiative.

Others have played an indirect but equally vital role by encouraging Vezina through the long years of democratic dissent: Jack and Mary Kirkland; Jim Harris, Chris Lea and other activists of the Green Party who set an awesome example of personal sacrifice and acceptance of legal risk in pursuit of political ideals; MP Simon deJong and staff in Ottawa, especially Adrian Morrison; Ontario PC leader Mike Harris and executive assistant Bill King; contributors to the legal fund; and the many lawyers of Gowling, Strathy and Henderson — the late Gordon Henderson, Ian Scott, Stephen Goudge, Ian McGilp, Martin Mason, Allen Reid, Martha Milczynski, Chris Dassios, Richard Stephenson and especially Malcolm Ruby, all of whom have provided fine advocacy for democracy over many years without sending impossible bills.

We acknowledge also the reading and critical comments of Tony Ruprecht, Peter Regenstreif, John Laschinger, Bob Vezina and Mark Emery. None of them, of course, bear any responsibility for the final result.

We thank Edward Nezic for keying the index on extremely short notice.

Finally we thank our wives, Cathy Pike and Kathy Kirkland Vezina for their patience and support during a hectic time and Kathy Vezina in particular for preparing the index.

John Deverell
Greg Vezina
Toronto
August 1993

FOREWORD

WHY DO MOST CANADIANS feel irritation when they watch their Members of Parliament and Senators in action? Why do we feel futility when we vote? Why can't we take any satisfaction from a $20-million royal commission on electoral reform or from this year's batch of vague promises of reform from stumping politicians? Why are they so incapable of leading us through the challenges of the 1990s to security and prosperity?

John Deverell and Greg Vezina in this book seek explanation by examining the underpinnings of our electoral democracy which, under their spotlight, turn out to be seriously defective. They argue that our democracy is a myth, a noble idea distorted by undemocratic rules for selecting Members or Parliament and forming governments. The result, they argue, is that we have no reliable method of getting the people we want to Parliament, little control over the formation of governments, and almost no idea what any party will do once it is in control.

In this political game a politician's first priority is getting elected, and his second priority is getting re-elected. This obsession distorts a politician's perspective and deflects him or her from concentrating on the task of providing good government. The constant campaigning and positioning for the next election makes our political parties reluctant to face the hard and sometimes unpopular choices needed to control government expenditure or reduce public bureaucracy.

In the last 40 years, as I built my auto parts company Magna International from a one-worker shop to an organization with 16,000 employees and $3 billion plus in annual sales, I have often departed from the conventional wisdom and found ways to get things done quicker and better. It is apparent that our democracy would benefit from some serious reorganization. Somehow our

Parliament must begin to behave more as the management team of the country and less as the forum for ritualized partisan shenanigans.

For years I have believed and argued that the needed shift in parliamentary behavior can be brought about by creating a non-partisan elected group of representatives to replace the Senate. My proposal for a strenghtened democracy calls for balancing the power of our political parties. We could do that by creating a group of elected representatives who aren't political and don't answer to parties. These new representatives would serve only one term, so their common priority would be smart government, not re-election.

If there were a hundred of these representatives (about the same number as we now have in the Senate), as a group they would hold a near-control position on parliamentary votes. Acting some-what like a jury, they could subject proposed legislation to a test of whether it was a good move the country could afford, or simply a shrewd move the governing party wanted.

A paramount feature of my recommendation would be random selection by a computer of about 20 candidates from the combined voters lists of two or three existing federal ridings. Those chosen who wanted to serve would each prepare a short resume listing work and residence history and what he or she would do for Canada. Resumes would be sent to all voters, with voting probably coinciding with other federal elections. Other campaigning by candidates or parties would be discouraged, although the media could be expected to develop information on candidates' backgrounds. The candidate winning the most votes would become the new representative for the combined ridings.

Deverell and Vezina make a strong case, however, that our methods for electing the House of Commons should not be left as they are. They suggest that political parties be represented in Parliament in direct proportion to their popular vote as is done in Germany and a number of other European countries, a change that would end Canada's tradition of single-party majority governments based on minority voter support. They also propose that Parliament share its power with the electorate by allowing citizens to challenge or initiate laws by petition and adopt or reject them by direct vote.

It is quite likely, as the book argues, that proportional representation voting will make party representation in Parliament less volatile from one election to another, and that greater continuity in Parliament will foster the serious long-term policy thinking the country needs from its elected leaders. But perhaps the most interesting feature of this book is that the authors do not limit themselves to putting forward a plausible theory of reform. They describe exactly how reform can be brought about if a significant number of Canadians decide they really want to see it happen.

As one of the many who are impatient with the excessively partisan focus of Canadian politics as now practised I welcome the controversy this work will stimulate. Deverell and Vezina deserve our gratitude for putting the debate about how to fix Ottawa and return democracy and prosperity to our future onto a different and more useful plane.

Frank Stronach
Markham, Ont.
August 1993

1

THE DEMOCRACY GAP

I want to change the way we do politics in this country.

— Kim Campbell, 1993, campaigning
to be leader of the
Progressive Conservative party
and Prime Minister of Canada

You had an option, sir.
You could have said: 'I'm not going to do it.
This is wrong for Canada
and I am not going to ask Canadians
to pay the price.' You had an option, sir,
to say no and you chose to say yes,
yes to the old attitudes and the old
stories of the Liberal Party.

— Brian Mulroney, 1984,
campaigning to be Prime Minister of Canada
by attacking Prime Minister John Turner
for patronage appointments

People don't want to talk about politics.
They don't trust politics any more.

— Nelson Reis, NDP House leader, 1993,
struggling to hold turf in British Columbia
threatened by the rise of the Reform Party

THE WAY WE DO POLITICS in this country, as the Prime Minister has pointed out, urgently needs to be changed. Most Canadians have known for the past 20 years that there is something badly amiss with our democracy, although on the spur of the moment we are hard pressed to explain why it works so poorly.

Accosted by a television reporter on the street corner or at home by a telephone pollster, most of us say that Canada would be better governed if only politicians were more honest, or if they were less controlled by their political parties and freer to do what "the people" want. These are emotional reactions which, on second thought, we know aren't going to get us out of the mess we're in. There may be momentary comfort in pretending that Canada can be run without political parties like some overgrown city council but we don't really believe it.

Our problem — the one that would let a political party registered as None Of The Above do very, very well in the upcoming federal election — is the diseased brand of party politics practised in this country. For nearly nine years we had a Prime Minister known far and wide as Lyin' Brian, but we know that the self-promoting Mulroney holds no monopoly on political mendacity. Misrepresentation, deception and broken promises are not aberrations in a Canadian political leader — they are part of the job description, the very essence of the Canadian political leadership style. When Canadians vote we may know the names of the people we're trying to put in office but that's about it. We've long since become accustomed to knowing nothing that really matters about their plans for the economy or for society — if indeed they have any of their own.

Those who think they know what our leaders stand for need to be reminded of the methods prime ministers have used to win office or cling to it in recent times. In 1974 inflation was the issue and Prime Minister Trudeau during the campaign ridiculed a Conservative proposal for wage controls. "Zap, you're frozen," he mocked. A year later Trudeau's government imposed wage controls. Joe Clark's Conservatives didn't boast about their plan to raise oil prices to world levels during the 1979 campaign but in office they tried it and then, facing the voters again unexpectedly in 1980, discovered what they already knew — we didn't like the idea. Trudeau didn't talk much about the Charter of Rights in that 1980 campaign — it came later when he was safely in office. In 1984 Mulroney's promise was "jobs, jobs, jobs" and the preservation of social programs which were, he assured us, a "sacred trust." The hacking at old age pensions and unemployment insurance started almost as soon as he took office. In 1984 Mulroney was also opposed to free trade, a Liberal scheme if ever there was one — but a year later he initiated free trade negotiations with the United States. During his terms of office Mulroney promised a massive adjustment program to help workers dislocated by free trade; the toughest conflict of interest bill in Canadian history; and a child care program that future generations would regard as the most important social innovation of the 1980s — none of which came to pass. In neither of the two Mulroney elections, 1984 and 1988, were we told that much of the Progressive Conservative party's sojourn in government would be expended trying to rewrite the constitution of Canada.

Our third established party, the NDP, has never governed in Ottawa so its federal leaders have had no opportunity to demonstrate their skills in the art of bamboozle and flip-flop. In Ontario, however, Premier Bob Rae has proved since 1990 that the New Democrats take a back seat to none of the other political dissemblers. Scarcely a week goes by without some sacred NDP cow being slain, mainly because the New Democrats over the decades in opposition accumulated a lot of unused policies and thus had more to renounce when they took up the tasks of government.

Our purpose here is not to pass judgment on the intrinsic merits of any of the surprise political retreats or surprise initiatives by the political parties. It is the common factor in all of them, the corrosive practice which subverts our democracy at its core, with which we are concerned: major policy choices are not presented to the electorate for prior approval. We the voters, who ought to be active participants in discussing, debating and setting the direction of government and society and then carrying out the democratically approved policies, are instead mere bystanders. Our fate as citizens is to applaud or condemn, once every four or five years, whatever stew the politicians have cooked up while they hold the reins of political power. Much of the anger, cynicism and mistrust which now permeates Canadian attitudes towards politics and politicians can be traced back to this gross defect in the way our democracy works — the effective exclusion of the mass of citizens from the main processes of decision-making.

Our argument in this book is that the Democracy Gap — the gulf between the weak, manipulative democracy we now have and what it realistically could be — can and should be overcome. We will show that much of the behavior Canadians so dislike in politicians results not from their character defects but from the inherent incentives for perverse behavior which accompany the British voting system — a feudal relic which we continue unthinkingly to inflict upon ourselves for no good reason. We will propose a series of reforms — in the voting system, in direct law-making, in the operation of government, and in televised election campaigning — which are needed to lift Canadian democracy out of its present lobotomized condition and give us the tools for effective democratic government in the twenty-first century. And we will outline a practical method by which ordinary Canadians, without the blessing of the political elites, can make these reforms happen.

There are alternatives to our proposals. We can decide, for example, to leave Canada's basic political arrangements undisturbed — but it will be difficult to do that now that their failings have spawned a government fiscal legacy that is harder and harder to live with. We can trust the Liberals, Progressive Conservatives and New Democrats to propose ways to restore public confidence in politics and government but, as we will show in Chapter Two, that's like assigning Dracula to guard the blood bank. We think that upon reflection most Canadians will share our judgment: the best hope for Canadian democracy is a new citizen's movement organised to pursue and compel changes in the most obnoxious features of our deformed political system. Here's what we need instead.

Open government. We need more openness and public participation in Ottawa's decision-making. The hegemony of the Prime Minister and the tradition of secret deals between cabinet ministers, top bureaucrats, lobbyists and provincial premiers must yield ground to Members of Parliament working in an effective House of Commons.

Direct democracy. The era of big public policy decisions without popular approval ended with the 1992 referendum on the Charlottetown Accord. From now on the electorate must be in a position to insist on referendums on constitutional change and major government policy initiatives such as wage and price controls, the national energy policy, free trade or the goods and services tax. We need a way for groups of citizens to directly initiate laws and bring them to a binding popular vote.

Electoral reform. Canada needs changes in election campaign rules and a switch from first-past-the-post or British voting rules to European-style proportional representation voting. A new voting system will provide for broader, fairer representation in Parliament, discourage the pathological promiscuity and unreliability of our political parties, and end what has proved to be a disastrous tradition of powerful, aimless, secretive one-party governments ruling without majority popular support.

THE MOOD OF THE PEOPLE

There is no question that the people of Canada are ready to consider changing the way politics is done. Keith Spicer's Citizens Forum on Canada's Future, despatched by the Prime Minister to lay the groundwork for what became the 1992 Charlottetown constitutional accord, returned to report "a fury in the land." Much of our anger was aimed at Mulroney himself, but clearly our discontents go well beyond one flawed and now-departed leader. Michael Adams, president of the Environics opinion research group, told the Council for Canadian Unity this spring that Canadians are "frustrated and anxious" as seldom before and have lost much of their respect for government institutions and leaders. The 1990s, he said, "will be characterized by a continuing demand for democratic reforms."

Chart 1.1
Confidence in Governments and Political Leaders

A Lot of / Some Confidence In (1976-1992)

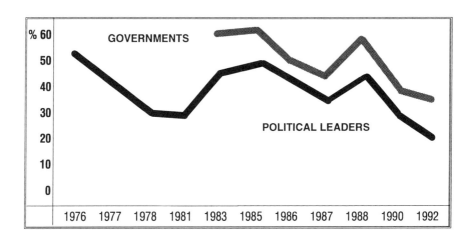

Chart 1.2
Approval of Leaders
(1988-1992)

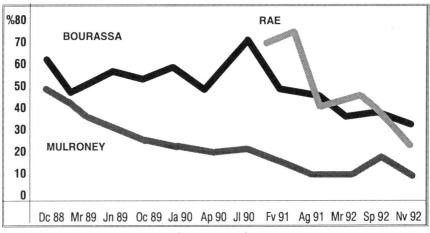

Source : Environics Research Group Ltd.

We in Canada are far more dissatisfied with our political institutions than the citizens of most modern democracies and even more dissatisfied than the Americans, whose democracy is also in urgent need of renovation. Nearly 40 per cent of Canadians said in 1992 that the federal government actually harms the public interest, and 32 per cent had the same low opinion of their provincial governments. The public discontent, in Adams' view, is related to dislocations in the Canadian economy and a shift "from the politics of prosperity to the politics of sacrifice." To put a point on it, prosperity allowed our political parties to provide poor leadership and supported enough public spending to lull us into complacency. The tougher competition and structural economic dislocations of the 1970s and 1980s, however, created fiscal pressures for the restructuring of government and government programs for which the parties were at first unprepared and which they remained reluctant to explain clearly to voters when facing election. The major public policy shift which has occured — for example the privatization of Air Canada and other public assets, the free trade agreement, and caps on federal transfer payments to provinces — has been organized by bureaucrats, by federal-provincial conferences, and by royal commissions with no explicit electoral mandates from the people of Canada. The people of Canada have noticed the oversight.

The election programs of Canadian political parties, one Parliament Hill veteran observes, have always been like ornaments on a Christmas tree: pretty, diverting and easily replaced.[1] The problem, in our view, is more serious. The Canadian electoral process has been so empty of basic policy choices that elections are the ornaments on the Christmas tree of state.

From his perch at Environics, Michael Adams says the only remedy for the growing gulf between citizens and government, as Canada's economic circumstances remain difficult, is more

---

1   Peter Dobell, director of the Parliamentary Centre for Foreign Affairs and Foreign Trade

democracy and more effective public involvement in the hard decisions which must be made. "The public now knows that elites can make massive mistakes," said Adams. "It wants the chance to make more decisions and accept responsibility for them."[2]

Surveys conducted for Canada's Royal Commission on Electoral Reform and Party Financing also confirm that many of us are deeply disturbed by the failings of our democratic electoral arrangements. "Canadians are demanding that electoral reform not merely tinker with the electoral law," reported royal commission chairman Pierre Lortie at the end of 1991. "They are demanding that it focus on the broader and central purposes of electoral democracy."[3] To questions about whether politicians care about voters, whether they lose touch with those who elect them, whether they're crooked, whether vast amounts of tax money are wasted, and whether the people running government are competent, Canadians are now giving more cynical answers than Americans. The only modern democracy in which citizens are more alienated from their governing institutions than we are is corrupt, Mafia-ridden Italy. While the hostile attitudes are expressed most strongly by women, immigrants and people with less formal education — the groups most underrepresented in Canadian government — they are shared by every large social grouping in every region of the country.[4] The commission's extensive polling identified among our concerns a "pervasive frustration with electoral outcomes" and "a perceived lack of responsiveness on the part of political parties."[5] The surveys showed well over half of us who have an opinion on the subject — 58 per cent —

---

2   Interview with the authors, May 1993
3   Lortie, Pierre et al., *Reforming Electoral Democracy*, Royal Commission on Electoral Reform and Party Financing (RC), Vol. 1, 1991, p.1
4   Ibid. p. 39
5   Fletcher, F. and Bakvis, H., RC Research, Vol. 17, preface

find it unacceptable that a political party can win a majority of seats in Parliament and form a majority government without winning a majority of the popular vote.[6] The same researchers found more than three-quarters of Canadians — 76 per cent — favorably disposed to an electoral model of the German type in which voters make two marks on their ballot — one for their preferred local candidate and one for their preferred national political party.[7] These surveys confirm our thesis that the public is willing to question the fundamental arrangements of the electoral system and the established party system and is well-disposed to reform proposals.

THE BROKERAGE POLITICS DISEASE

The British voting system used in Canada is part of the living room furniture, so familiar that we overlook the insidious and poisonous influence it exercises on our politics. Also known as the first-past-the-post election system and the single member plurality system, it consists of three electoral rules — one ballot per voter, one elected representative per constituency, and the candidate with the most votes wins. This voting system has two major defects which have not been fatal to it in Canada, but should be. It is inherently unfair because it wastes the vote and negates the party preference of every citizen who doesn't choose a winning candidate — generally the majority of the electorate. It also requires parties serious about winning to adopt unprincipled and ultimately destructive behaviors and strategies.

The political scientists who conduct Canada's National Election Study, a systematic scrutiny of Canadian voting behavior from election to election, have described and tried to explain the dismal, tenuous relationship between Canadian voters and the politi-

---

6   Blais, André and Gidengil, Elizabeth. *Making Representative Democracy Work: The View of Canadians,* 1991, RC Research, Vol. 17, p. 54
7   Ibid. p. 56

cal parties.[8] They warn at the outset that the mandate theory of representative government — the notion that elections allow political parties to present projects describing their intentions for the future, that voters choose among the projects, and that parties adjust their positions slowly and carefully over time to avoid confusing voters about what they stand for — is completely useless as an explanation of what goes on in Canadian politics.

> For such evaluation to work the parties themselves must provide a relatively fixed point of reference, some predictability to their behavior, and some consistency between words and actions. The lack of fixity, predictability and consistency in Canadian political parties has led observers for decades to characterize them as brokers.... In each election the parties canvas and delineate the varied interests of the electorate in a process of coalition-creation or brokering.[9]

The voting system has not encouraged Canadian political parties to adopt principled positions or to cultivate reliable voter allegiances in the manner common to European parliamentary democracies where proportional representation voting allows for a diverse party system. Instead the Canadian parties all try to be all things to all people. They are locked in a cutthroat game in which each tries to court a voting majority, relatively few extra votes can confer a large majority in Parliament, and relatively small shortfalls can lead to sudden oblivion. Under those conditions it has always been perilous for Canadian political parties to present policy in other than general and innocuous terms, and has made the electoral discussion of large, ambitious, or controversial ideas impolitic. Instead we have Santa Claus political parties specialized in the distribution of election goodies — the budget-busting gifts and promises, usually with clear short-term payoffs and unexplained long-term costs, which Canadian parties offer to different regions of the country, different producer groups and different seg-

---

8   Clarke, Harold and Jane Jenson, Lawrence LeDuc, Jon Pammett. *Absent Mandate: Interpreting Change in Canadian Elections*, 1991
9   Ibid. p. 9

ments of the electorate in their ceaseless pursuit of an elusive goal — single-party majority government.

Some of the deceptive party behavior arises from the presumption that national parties must try not only to win majorities, but to win majorities in each region of the country and in particular in French-speaking Quebec. As political scientist David Elkins put it, "because we do not have a nation in the strict sense, but two nations or none, we expect the parties to paper over the fundamental cleavages."[10] In most countries political parties take opposite sides of fundamental social cleavages — religion, language, social class — and represent those interests in the legislature, which is where the necessary political compromises are reached. In Canada the anti-politics presumption has been that each political party must assemble a coalition of interests diverse enough to represent the entire country in a majority government. This sets a very difficult task for two parties and an impossible one for three or more, but that doesn't stop them from trying.

The peculiar Canadian tradition of political brokerage goes all the way back to Prime Minister John A. Macdonald, who incorporated French and English, Protestant and Catholic within his Conservative party and held the whole disparate melange together with "side-payments" — patronage. The brokerage style was later imitated successfully by Sir Wilfrid Laurier at the head of the Liberal Party. By extensive use of the pork barrel

...the two major parties usurped some of Parliament's historic functions and contributed to its lessened status.... The crucial point here is that brokerage was originally a parliamentary function but that it became a party function in Canada.... We have not trusted Parliament to do its job and we have then asked another institution to remedy the defect.[11]

---

10 Elkins, David. Parties as National Institutions, RC Research, Vol. 14, p. 13
11 Ibid. p. 29

The old brokerage system outlived its usefulness 70 years ago when new regionally-based ideological parties — the Progressives, the Cooperative Commonwealth Federation, and Social Credit — rose up to challenge the alternation of Liberals and Conservatives in government. The traditional parties sustained the old game long beyond its time only by expanding the scope of brokerage payments enormously, harnessing federal taxing and spending powers "to buy off entire groups and regions. The cost of these latter measures accounts in large part for the debilitating deficits and accumulated debt of recent federal governments."[12]

The fiscal distress of the Canadian state is attributable in large measure to the pathological brokerage style of Canadian political competition. We will show in Chapter Three that the only efficient way to end the grand, misdirected conceits of the parties and get the task of reconciling Canada's differences into Parliament where it belongs is to knock away the rotten prop on which the brokerage game depends — British voting rules.

Once the voting rules are changed, the political parties will find their promiscuous brokerage routines irrelevant. They will become smaller parties with more sharply-defined images, clearer ideologies and programs, and stronger ties to reliable groups of voters. In other words, they will be more like European political parties. We will no longer see parties operating such a huge tent as the Liberals were in 1968 when two Blue Grits, Robert Winters and John Turner, between them won almost as many votes for the Liberal leadership as the winner, Pierre Trudeau. The same Liberal party under different voting rules would probably have taken a much closer look at Jean Chrétien in 1984 instead of making him wait until 1990. Similarly the Progressive Conservatives under sensible voting rules would probably revert to calling themselves the Conservative Party and would be unlikely to choose a Red Tory like Joe Clark to carry the party banner.

---

12   Ibid. p. 45

These new, slimmed down and more principled political parties would do for Canadian voters what parties are supposed to do, and what ours fail to do. In our current voting system, most individual voters have no direct influence on election outcomes and thus little enough reason to take their vote seriously. Parties should be sufficiently predictable that the party label gives voters a quick, efficient way of knowing what to expect from politicians on major ideological questions — whether the means of production should be publicly or privately owned, whether government should play an extended or limited role in planning the economy, whether there should be more or less redistribution of wealth from the rich to the poor, and whether social programs should be expanded or cut back. Our political parties instead make it their business to obscure these distinctions and make rational voting as difficult as possible.

> Canadian parties are most comfortable multiplying the number of politically relevant divisions (among the voters).... Commonly they make appeals to narrow interests and proposals that tinker with existing arrangements. Rather than follow through on the logic of stances developed in the past, brokerage parties practise inconsistency as they search for electorally successful formulae or respond to new versions of old problems.... A wide variety of conflicting and contradictory policy stances may co-exist inside each brokerage party. [13]

This style of electoral competition can produce good government only by accident. The political parties, competing on many fronts for the same voters, start each election from remarkably small bases of established and reliable voter support — much smaller than popular vote statistics suggest, because the apparent minimum figures for each party in elections and opinion polls conceal an astounding flux of vote-switching in all directions. In 1988, for example, the Progressive Conservatives had the largest

---

13   Clarke, H. et al., op. cit., p. 10

core support at 13 per cent of the electorate. The Liberal core vote was only 9 per cent, and the New Democratic Party could count absolutely on only 6 per cent of the voters.[14] Canadian voters and the rootless Canadian political parties are, in the lingo of the political scientists, permanently dealigned. Volatility, uncertainty and negative attitudes are what Canadian elections are all about as shallow political parties pursue shallow, temporary relationships with voters who long for something better and never find it.

The National Election Studies show that in any given election two-thirds of voters are available to all parties and an astonishing one-third, give or take a few percentage points, will switch from the party they supported the last time. To reach these floating voters the parties are forever discovering problems, or new aspects of problems, and presenting themselves and their leaders as competent purveyors of the quick fix.

> Political issues pour forth in profusion...yet the shelf life of issues is short. Some are tossed away, while others are grabbed up greedily by a waiting public seeking sustenance. Despite the seeming generosity of the servings, the public is often hungry again.... Programs, being longer term in nature, are not often acknowledged by the parties during election campaigns. Potentially attractive elements from them are, however, introduced as election issues. The common pattern is for larger programs to be ignored during elections and then brought forward immediately afterward. The National Energy Program, the Free Trade Agreement and tax reform are three recent examples about which electoral discussion was muted at best.... Issues moved onto the electoral stage during the 1970s and 1980s in every way except that which democratic theory implies is the most appropriate. In no case was an important project deliberately announced as a lead up to an election campaign and a mandate sought to carry it out....[15]

---

14   Ibid. p. 53
15   Ibid. p. 73

Chart 1.3
Thermometer Scale Ratings of Party Leaders,
1968-88

>50 is better,   <50 is worse   50 = neutral

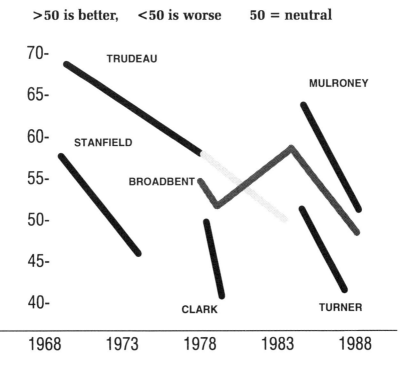

Source: Harold Clarke et al, *Absent Mandate*. It should be noted that Pierre Trudeau was no longer PM when the 1984 poll was taken.

Brokerage parties identify problems such as inflation or un-employment and avoid specific, controversial commitments by declaring their general competence to deal with them. The practice places a heavy burden on the image of the party leader, a phenomenon further exaggerated by the dominant role of television in election campaigning. The party leaders are the anchors of the brokerage system but also its major casualties as the public becomes aware ever more quickly that the projected competence, quick fixes and band-aids they traffic in are illusory. As the brokerage party system falters there is a tendency for the shelf life of leaders to become almost as short as the shelf life of issues.

This summer as the election period approached the Progressive Conservative government was experimenting with an old brokerage party tactic — a new leader. Prime Minister Kim Campbell's very traditional task was to help the voters forget the party record and their desire to hold her predecessor, Brian Mulroney, to account. To perform this feat Campbell was contemplating something radically new. Not only would she promise to balance the federal budget by 1998, but she was thinking of actually telling Canadians in advance how she would do it. After years of squeezing government overhead and freezing program spending without getting the annual deficit below $30 billion, some insiders were telling Campbell that the government had no choice left but to announce chops in politically sensitive areas — native programs, unemployment insurance, defence, old age security and provincial transfers — and to allow deterrent fees for "non-essential" medical services. The idea of campaigning on specific cutback proposals is so utterly foreign to Canadian electoral tradition that it admits of only one interpretation. Some influential Conservatives, aware that Campbell's personal acceptability could not overcome the party's terrible deficit in popular appeal, had already written off the 1993 election and were trying to build a platform for opposition and a little credibility for a resurrection next time around.

By late summer the fit of madness passed and Campbell, apparently entertaining hopes of victory induced by her own party's manipulated public opinion polls, made it clear that she would not spell out specific budget cuts during the election campaign. Certainly the spring polling information coming out of Environics had given Campbell and her colleagues no cause for optimism. It indicated that the Conservative Party, had an election been held in

Table 1.1

Question: Here is a list of the federal political parties in Canada.[16] If all of these parties had candidates running in your riding, and if a Canadian federal election were held today, which one of these parties would you vote for?

	TOTAL	ATL.	QUE.	ONT.	MAN.	SASK.	ALTA.	B.C.
SAMPLE (decided)	1514	183	398	428	89	92	152	172
LIBERAL	38	47	22	50	39	24	34	37
PROGRESSIVE CONSERVATIVE	19	21	15	20	19	13	28	19
BLOC QUÉBÉCOIS	13	-	46	-	-	-	-	-
NDP	11	8	4	11	20	36	9	13
REFORM	8	5	-	9	7	18	20	17
OTHER	10	9	12	8	12	8	9	12

Source: Environics Research Group Ltd. Focus Canada Report 1993-2

---

16   This survey for the first time explicitly named 12 registered political parties including the Rhinoceros Party, Green Party, Family Coalition Party, Social Credit Party, National Party, Libertarian Party, and Communist Party. The "Other" category leaped from 2 per cent in the previous survey to 10 per cent.

June, would have been beaten badly in every province of Canada and reduced from majority status to a rump smaller than the Bloc Québécois. Only 25 per cent of the respondents were undecided.

Aside from the evisceration of the Conservative Party the poll showed the Bloc Québécois poised for a sweep of Quebec on less than half the vote, the New Democratic Party in serious difficulty everywhere except Saskatchewan, the Reform Party too low to elect more than a few members and the Liberals, on a 38 per cent vote, positioned for a big majority government with few Quebec members.[17] The very possibility of a parliamentary outcome which departs so drastically from voter intentions is proof beyond a reasonable doubt that British voting rules thwart our efforts at rational politics. As we try to drive the sedan of Canadian democracy we find that not only does the front seat face backwards but the steering wheel is disconnected. Parties blind us to the future by failing to plan and concealing their few serious intentions, and then the electoral system makes nonsense of our attempts to indicate which people and parties we want in Parliament. The warranty on this machine promises nothing but an unpredictable and bumpy ride.

This fall well over half of all Canadian voters will realize, as soon as the vote is counted, that their ballot had absolutely no effect on Parliament. Surplus votes for candidates who win are un-

---

17   By August Angus Reid was reporting support for the Progressive Conservative Party in the 30 per cent range but this is more a reflection of polling technique than of volatility in public opinion. First, Canadians do not always tell pollsters the truth, especially during telephone interviews. Second, results can be strongly skewed by the structure of questioning. The in-home interview poll on which we relied made no mention of party leaders but asked for voting intention. A pollster seeking to boost the Tory numbers, and knowing that respondents like to seem consistent, can ask them first whether they think Kim Campbell or Jean Chrétien will make a better prime minister. Because Campbell does well on that question, a later question on party preference is likely to show more support for the Conservatives than is actually there. The final poll, the big one, will shed more light on the accuracy of the two polling methods and provide further insight on whether Canadians vote primarily for parties or for leaders.

necessary and, in that sense, will have been wasted. More seriously, the large number of votes cast for all losing candidates — the
lost legions of the Reform Party, the New Democratic Party, the
Progressive Conservative Party, the National Party, the Green Party
and even the Liberal Party in Quebec — will have absolutely no
impact on the election result. The minority in English-speaking
Canada which votes Liberal will be massively overrepresented.
The Bloc Québécois, which wants to break up Confederation, is
likely to be massively overrepresented. It is little wonder that
Canadian voters feel powerless. It's because under such perverse
voting rules most of us are powerless.

THE ESTABLISHED PARTY GAME:
DISTORTED REPRESENTATION

The defects of the voting system are as old as Confederation. In
Canada's election system the two dominant federal parties, the
Liberals and Progressive Conservatives, have always gambled for a
prize which either can win and neither usually deserves: exclusive
control of the government of Canada, its powers, its favors, and its
patronage. Over the long haul the two big parties have been alter-
nately successful in their pursuit of majorities in Parliament but
those partisan victories have almost always been tainted by the
fact that they rest on minority popular support. They violated
what should be the cardinal rule of our democracy: all voters are
equal, and majority rules. Most of the time Canadians are
governed, not by Members of Parliament representing majority
opinion, but by the party of the largest minority.

Sometimes the electoral system delivers an outcome even more
capricious than usual. In 1896, for example, with only two large
parties contesting the election, Sir Wilfrid Laurier's Liberals won a
Parliamentary majority with fewer votes than their Conservative
opponents. In 1979 Joe Clark's Conservatives won the largest number of seats in Parliament and formed a government with a popular
vote substantially lower than the vote of the Liberals. Many of our
provincial legislatures provide even more extreme examples of distorted and unfair representation. In Quebec, for example, Robert

Table 1.2 — Distorted Representation:
Canadian Federal Elections 1878-1988*
(percentages)

Year	CONSERVATIVE		LIBERAL		OTHERS	
	Vote	Seats	Vote	Seats	Vote	Seats
1878	**50.7**	**60.9**	46.8	33.6	2.5	0.5
1887	**50.2**	**58.6**	48.7	41.4	1.1	0.0
1891	**51.1**	**56.3**	47.1	43.7	1.8	0.0
1896	46.1	41.3	45.1	**55.4**	8.9	3.3
1900	47.4	37.6	**51.2**	**62.4**	1.3	0.0
1904	46.4	35.0	**52.0**	**64.5**	1.5	0.5
1908	46.8	38.5	**50.4**	61.1	2.7	0.5
1911	**50.9**	60.6	47.7	39.4	1.3	0.0
1917	**57.0**	**65.1**	39.9	34.9	3.1	0.0
1921	30.3	21.3	40.7	49.4	29.0	29.2
1925	46.5	47.3	39.9	40.4	13.7	12.2
1926	45.3	37.1	46.1	**52.2**	8.7	10.6
1930	48.8	**55.9**	45.2	37.1	6.0	6.9
1935	29.6	16.3	44.8	**70.6**	25.5	13.1
1940	30.7	16.3	51.5	**73.9**	17.8	9.8
1945	27.4	27.3	40.9	**51.0**	31.8	21.5
1949	29.7	15.6	49.5	**73.7**	20.9	10.7
1953	31.0	19.2	48.8	**64.5**	20.3	16.3
1957	38.9	42.3	40.9	39.6	20.1	18.1
1958	**53.6**	**78.5**	33.6	18.5	12.8	3.0
1962	37.3	43.8	37.2	37.7	25.6	18.5
1963	32.8	35.8	41.7	48.7	25.4	15.5
1965	32.4	36.6	40.2	49.4	27.5	14.0
1968	31.4	27.3	45.5	**58.7**	23.1	14.0
1972	35.0	40.5	38.5	41.3	26.5	18.2
1974	35.4	36.0	43.2	**53.4**	21.4	10.7
1979	35.9	48.2	40.1	40.4	24.0	11.3
1980	32.5	36.5	44.3	**52.1**	23.3	11.3
1984	**50.0**	**74.8**	28.0	14.2	22.9	11.0
1988	43.0	**57.3**	31.9	28.1	25.1	14.6

* The figures show the percentage of the total vote attracted by each party and the percentage of House of Commons seats won. Bold type indicates a majority. Source: Mackie, T. and Rose, R., *The International Almanac of Electoral History*, 1991, pp. 66-87.

Bourassa's Liberals crushed Rene Lévesque and the Parti Québécois in 1973, taking 93 per cent of the seats in the Quebec National Assembly and leaving only 5.5 per cent for the PQ. The Liberal landslide was based on 54.7 per cent of the popular vote while the 30.2 per cent of the population which voted for the PQ was almost entirely unrepresented. That spectacular inequity stimulated discussion of electoral reform in Quebec but the separatist party lost its zeal for the idea after winning its first majority government on a very thin vote in 1976.

In Alberta the Progressive Conservatives led by Peter Lougheed won 95 per cent of the seats in the 1982 election on 62 per cent of the popular vote, maintaining that province's long tradition of absurdly lopsided legislatures. The 19.2 per cent of the population which chose Alberta's New Democrats saw their party win only 2.5 per cent of the seats. In the most recent Saskatchewan election Roy Romanow's NDP captured 83 per cent of the legislature with 51 per cent of the vote. The Liberal Party, with support of 23 per cent of voters, won just one seat. In British Columbia the New Democrats led by Mike Harcourt received almost twice as many votes as Social Credit — and seven times as many seats. Frank McKenna's Liberals in New Brunswick achieved the ultimate in overrepresentation in 1987, translating 60 per cent of the popular vote into 100 per cent control of the provincial legislature. The unrepresented 40 per cent of the population was supposed to be consoled by McKenna's decision to allow opposition parties to send written questions into the legislature. In June this year the nation was told that Ralph Klein, the former mayor of Calgary, had performed a miracle by saving the discredited Alberta Conservative dynasty and returning it to office with 62 per cent of the seats in the Alberta legislature, in the process wiping the Alberta New Democrats off the map. The Klein "political miracle" was based on a 45 per cent popular vote in a three-party contest.

In federal politics the extreme distortions in party representation have occured at a regional level and feed resentments which endanger Canada's survival as a federation. During the 1970s Pierre Trudeau's Liberals, despite substantial popular support in the West, were unable to elect candidates west of Winnipeg and Trudeau resorted to appointing Senators as ministers to keep some westerners at his cabinet table. The Liberal Prime Minister toyed with the idea of electoral reform but did not proceed, probably because a full-fledged voting reform would have undercut the Liberal hegemony in Quebec which had been the key to so many majority governments. Trudeau's calculation, in effect, was that Liberal voters in Western Canada would have to continue unrepresented so that Conservative and NDP voters in Quebec could continue unrepresented. For decades, except for one election in 1958, Quebec remained an electoral desert for the Conservative Party and it has continued to be a desert for the New Democrats. The Conservative Party did not call for electoral reform, however, preferring to wait as long as necessary for a major shift in Quebec opinion to provide it with a basis for majority government. The change finally occurred in 1984.

The Liberal and Conservative parties have always given top priority to maintaining a shot — for the Conservatives usually a long shot — at single-party control of Parliament and the pork barrel. Their goal requires the perpetuation of British voting rules, and so we still have them. The resulting lousy pattern of regional representation within federal governments, and the dominant role of Prime Ministers and MPs from Quebec in both Liberal and Conservative governments, have been major destabilizing factors in Canadian politics. Even so, we are not surprised when senior Liberal and Conservative politicians cling like barnacles to a system which grants them more power than the voters are willing to confer. What is more puzzling, at least at first blush, is the posture of a smaller party like the New Democratic Party which has little or no hope of playing a constructive role in national government under existing election rules and yet defends the status quo. The paradox quickly dissolves when we take into account the domain of provincial government where the NDP wields legislative majorities or forms the official opposition in four provinces with more than half Canada's population. The federal NDP and its provincial parties in Alberta, Quebec, New Brunswick, Nova Scotia, Prince Edward Island and Newfoundland, clearly need

Table 1.3
Distorted Regional Representation in Four Elections
(percentages)

	CONSERVATIVE		LIBERAL		NDP	
	Quebec					
	Vote	Seats	Vote	Seats	Vote	Seats
1979	13.5	2.7	**61.7**	**89.3**	5.1	0.0
1980	12.6	1.3	**68.2**	**98.7**	9.1	0.0
1984	**50.2**	**77.3**	35.4	22.7	8.8	0.0
1988	**52.7**	**84.0**	30.2	16.0	14.0	0.0
	Western Canada					
1979	49.6	**74.0**	22.6	3.8	29.7	22.0
1980	46.8	**63.6**	23.4	2.6	28.3	33.7
1984	**50.4**	**75.3**	15.6	2.6	27.5	22.0
1988	41.1	**55.8**	20.3	7.0	29.6	37.2

electoral reform. They have been sacrificed so New Democrats in British Columbia, Saskatchewan, Manitoba and Ontario may pursue the thrill — and spoils — of undeserved majority goverment.[18]

Similarly, the federal Liberal and Conservative parties have been willing to sacrifice various provincial organizations rather than switch

---

18   Former NDP leader Ed Broadbent put forward a proposal for proportional representation voting for the federal Parliament in 1978 but was unable to persuade NDP provincial leaders to take up the cause and so had to drop it.

to a European-style electoral system which allows the electorate a complete menu of political choice. In Quebec there is no provincial Conservative Party to speak of. For years until Laurence Decore's breakthrough no Liberal was elected to the Alberta legislature. In Saskatchewan either the Liberal party or the Conservative party is usually put to sleep to allow anti-NDP forces to rally under a single banner. In British Columbia the tradition, until it collapsed before the last election, was to starve both traditional parties and unite the free enterprise vote in the Social Credit party to keep the NDP out of office.

THE UNFETTERED MANDATE

The goal of our established political parties, assisted by the voting rules, is to acquire a parliamentary majority and with it an unfettered mandate to govern. Pierre Trudeau did it in 1968, riding vague musings about participatory democracy straight into the prime minister's office after just three years in Parliament. His Liberals captured 59 per cent of the seats in Parliament, a comfortable majority, with the support of just 45.5 per cent of the voters. Brian Mulroney grabbed political power even more decisively in 1984 after winning the leadership of the Conservative party without ever sitting in Parliament. He parlayed the support of 50 per cent of Canada's voters into an overwhelming parliamentary majority with 75 per cent of the seats in the House of Commons. The Conservatives then maintained firm control of Parliament in 1988 despite a sharp drop in voter support to 43 per cent.

Once in office Canadian prime ministers heading majority governments are autocrats, setting policy and dispensing patronage on their own terms for four or five years until the next election. The prime minister is within our political system far more powerful than the president of the United States in theirs.

The prime minister has enormous personal powers to appoint and dismiss ministers and parliamentary secretaries and to strongly influence a vast array of order-in-council appointments; to largely control the committee process by means of appointments and determination of budgets and staff; to largely determine the cabinet agenda; and so on.[19]

Prime ministers are always consequential in parliamentary systems but ours derive extra clout from being party leaders elected at convention, which puts them beyond the control of their parliamentary colleagues.[20] Defenders of the autocracy say it may not be theoretically elegant but it produces strong, stable government. Native-born Canadians imbibe the "strong and stable" mantra in the public schools if they don't get it with their mother's milk. Newcomers, if they notice the problem, are expected to accept it as the Canadian way. As Brian Mulroney put it recently, a "duly elected" government has a "mandate to govern" which in his view includes the right to take measures opposed by the population. "You can be, these days, a popular prime minister or an effective one. You can't be both," Mulroney said. Brian Mulroney may be gone but the Mulroney Doctrine — that a prime minister in command of a parliamentary majority can do whatever he can get away with — is still very much with us, entrenched in the rules of our electoral system.

A SAD TRADITION: NEGATIVE VOTING

The only defense Canadians now have against surprise attacks by the prime minister is to wait for an election and throw the rascal out. Politicians for their part try to enact unpopular surprise

---

19   Stanbury, W.T. *Business-Government Relations in Canada*, 1986, p. 132
20   Both Margaret Thatcher, long the dominant figure in British politics, and her predecessor Ted Heath, were driven from the leadership of the British Conservative Party in a matter of weeks by revolts in the Conservative parliamentary caucus. A British Prime Minister is powerful but not invincible. No British party leader can ignore the lesson.
      In Australia and New Zealand, Prime Ministers from the Labour Party are somewhat constrained by a tradition in which the sitting party members elect the cabinet.

measures early in their term of office in the hope that we will for-give or forget before the next ballot, and they often win that gamble. Sometimes, however, there is a popular consensus not just that a government doesn't deserve to remain in office — after all, most of us didn't vote for it in the first place — but that our next ballot must be marked for the sole purpose of defeating the government. This requires many of us, under British voting rules, to abandon the parties which best represent our political views. To bring the government to account it is not sufficient to deny it our votes. We are driven to vote for the candidate in our riding who has the best chance to beat the governing party's candidate.

The great significance of negative voting is captured in the oft-repeated aphorism: "Opposition parties don't win elections. Governments lose them." What the aphorism doesn't reveal is the stupefying effect of negative voting on our entire political culture. The negative balloting may accomplish its purpose, a rude good-bye to prime minister and governing cabal, but the unintended consequences are drastic. In the same fell swoop it confers on the leader of the other dominant party an unfettered parliamentary majority which, if it isn't really what voters wanted, contributes further to the climate of political cynicism. The negative voting also sideswipes and slaughters alternative parties, driving their ac-tivists to despair and flushing their creative energies out of the body politic.

There is only one kind of alternative political party which is al-lowed to survive under British voting rules — a party with enough geographically concentrated support to be a dominant party in some constituencies. Parties of ideas with significant but diffuse support — the Greens, the National Party, Reform and for many years the NDP — are put in mortal danger by the voting rules under which they are trying to compete. The Bloc Québécois, by contrast, is in a position to profit from the voting rules. Its no-con-tent appeal for regional solidarity among French-speaking Quebecers may make it the official voice of Quebec while more than half the province's citizens vote for other parties and get little or no representation.

The effect of British voting rules, and the explicit intent of those who defend them, is to suffocate independent-minded democratic debate and force all serious political activity to pass through the swamp of the large brokerage parties. Generally this is exactly what happens, but there is one kind of dissent the rules cannot manage — dissent based on deeply felt claims of regional grievance or, in the case of Quebec, regional-linguistic grievance. This type of dissent, when it becomes strong enough, is suddenly encouraged and overamplified by the voting rules. Both these features of the electoral system — the suppression and the over-amplification — are deeply perverse. Our democracy is strangling on its own dysfunctional rules, and the immediate task of real democrats from all parties and all walks of life is to join in a swift rescue operation.

2

BLIND ALLEY:
THE OFFICIAL REFORMS

CANADA'S POLITICAL ELITES know they must address the public's unsettled mood by promising to do something about our failing political system. As the Lortie Royal Commission on Electoral Reform and Party Financing stated in 1991 the official cure should address the "broad and central purposes of electoral democracy" but the established parties have found that idea too dangerous. Instead proposals for minor tinkering are sprouting everywhere.

Liberal leader Jean Chrétien seemed to acknowledge in January that the House of Commons is comatose by unveiling a plan for "Reviving Parliamentary Democracy." He called his proposals for changes to election rules and to procedures of the House of Commons "a comprehensive package for reforming Canada's political institutions." Canadians "feel alienated from their political institutions and they want to restore integrity to them," said Chrétien. The Liberals, however, had the scent of majority government in their nostrils and didn't want to change the electoral rules in any way that might jeopardize their turn at the public trough. Their proposed electoral changes consisted of higher election spending limits, restricted election advertising by groups other than political parties, and higher public subsidies for parties which elect more women candidates.

Prime Minister Kim Campbell, when she was pursuing the Conservative leadership this spring, set out a plan for "democratic reform" aimed almost entirely at the internal procedures of the Conservative party. "Doing Politics Differently" for Campbell means only one specific change in the broader electoral system — a permanent voters list which will allow for shorter election campaigns. This is right in line with the thinking which led the Conservative party to wait five years for an election — that the only way to please Canadian voters is to expose them to campaigning politicians as little as possible. In August, allowing that "for many Canadians Ottawa is a place where politicians go to play power games or to line their pockets," Campbell suggested some possible changes in parliamentary pensions, lobbying rules and the distribution of patronage appointments.

The very skimpiness of the major party proposals indicates that the politicians, while ready to flap their gums about reform, expect to endure high levels of public disapproval on a continuing basis and carry on business much as usual. Experience has taught the political elite that when all parties in the House of Commons maintain a common front on the basic rules of the political game there's not much voters can do about it.

This assessment of what the three parties are up to is confirmed by comparing their modest proposals with the extensive recommendations of the Lortie royal commission on electoral reform and also by the actions of a special House of Commons committee on electoral reform this spring. There, after a number of secret sessions, the parties agreed to ignore much of the royal commission's report.[1]

The royal commission, appointed in 1989 by Prime Minister Brian Mulroney, was spearheaded by Pierre Lortie, a rising Montreal business executive associated with the Provigo grocery chain before his political tour of duty and now safely back in the private sector at the top level of the Bombardier group. It represents a best effort by thoughtful Liberals, Conservatives and New Democrats to dress up the first-past-the-post electoral system and

---

1   Leslie Seidle, the royal commission's senior research co-ordinator, told fellow political scientists at a learned societies meeting that the Commons committee's *in camera* hatchet work was "an outrageous abuse of the democratic process."

the operations of the brokerage parties it has shaped to make them more publicly acceptable. Among the seasoned partisans who worked with Lortie on the exercise were Lucie Pepin for the Liberals, Elwood Cowley and Bill Knight for the NDP, and Conservatives Don Oliver, Pierre Fortier and Robert Gabor. Over the course of two years, and at a public cost of nearly $20 million, they prepared a detailed plan to help their parties and Parliament rebuild credibility. "Our goal," said the final report, "was to enhance the legitimacy of the Canadian House of Commons and of our institutions of governance. Legitimacy is a most important resource, if only for the economy it allows in the use of all the others." In a bid to speed them into effect in time for this year's election, the commissioners took the unusual extra step of presenting all their recommendations as draft legislation. Their delusions of influence were soon shattered, however, and it became clear that the party leaders had no intention of taking the proposed reforms seriously let alone fast-tracking them.

In retrospect Lortie's commission appears to have been doomed from the beginning by decisions taken in the prime minister's office. The official terms of reference were "to inquire into and report on the appropriate principles and process that should govern the election of members of the House of Commons and the financing of political parties and of candidates' campaigns." That ruled out recommendations on Senate reform, which is one avenue for dealing with issues of regional representation in Parliament. It also excluded any consideration of sharing Parliament's legislative powers directly with the voters. But the most critical omission of all was one not required by the written terms of reference. Lortie accepted his assignment from Prime Minister Mulroney on the understanding that the commission would not study or recommend European-style proportional representation as a remedy for the disorders of Canada's parliamentary system.

As Mulroney once said on the subject of loyalty: "You gotta dance with the guy what brung you." In this case the prime minister took the precept beyond the personal and showed loyalty to the voting rules and party system which had made it possible for him to rule Canada for nine years, first with a popular majority and then without one. A system that had served Brian Mulroney and his anonymous financial backers so well obviously did not need fundamental change. Mulroney's understanding with Lortie was quickly adopted by the Liberals and New Democrats in the first meetings of the commission and cast its pall over all subsequent proceedings. It was a continuing embarrassment to the academic research team as many of the dozens of political scientists invited in for consultations expressed amazement at the commission's deliberate self-blinkering.[2]

Still, Lortie sustained his end of the deal to the end. The political decision stands, naked and unelaborated, in the opening section of the report:

> We recommend that the current representational system, with members of the House of Commons selected from single member constituencies based on the plurality of votes cast in a constituency, be maintained.

There are, broadly speaking, only two routes to substantial change in the way Canada's parliamentary system works. One is proportional representation, the avenue Mulroney, Lortie and the other party representatives ruled out in advance with those few words. The other is the path chosen by Lortie and reflected in his report — a major state intervention in the internal life of the established political parties in the hope of making them more open and democratic, combined with other legal pressures to make all competing political interests operate within the framework of those parties.

Lortie justified his single-track approach by claiming insider knowledge. He, the practical businessman, intended to make proposals which would be acceptable to Prime Minister Mulroney and the other politicians in power — recommendations which could quickly become law and affect the real world.[3] As it turned out the prime minis-

---

2   Authors' interview with York University professor Fred Fletcher, co-ordinator of the commission's research on politics and media.
3   Interview with Deverell during public hearings in Toronto

ter did not endorse Lortie's blueprint for party reform and instead left it to the mercy of a Commons committee. The royal commission chairman refused telephone calls and has offered no public comment on the House of Commons decision this spring to bury his work, which makes it hard to establish exactly where and how his pragmatic strategy became impractical. From a public point of view, however, it makes little difference whether the worldly businessman was suckered and then double-crossed by Mulroney the political manipulator, or whether Lortie knew from the beginning he was part of a political fraud. Either way Canadians are left with no democratic reform and a pricey set of tax-financed research documents which are heavily slanted toward Lortie's preconceived ideas.

Even though Lortie discouraged the discussion of proportional representation, however, the idea proved too potent to ignore. The research papers and even the commission's final report keep sneaking bits and pieces of it through the back door because it is the only sensible approach to fair and democratic representation. Before describing Lortie's repeated lapses into PR heresy, however, we must provide a summary of what the royal commissioners found wrong with the first-past-the-post electoral regime and its brokerage parties and the improvements they proposed.

THE MAXIMUM OFFICIAL REFORM PACKAGE

Lortie's detailed scheme to save the political status quo had three main elements: an increase in public funding to major parties tied to new laws to open up and regulate their internal life; a party monopoly on political advertising during election campaigns; and sops and buyoffs to the various groups denied any realistic hope of seats in the House of Commons by the rejection of proportional representation. The credibility of this package, Lortie realized, required the adoption of all its elements. In particular he knew that the attempt to silence all private interest groups during election campaigns is hard to justify under the Charter of Rights but might be defensible if voters are able to acquire information from and choose among a variety of open, democratic parties which together can reasonably claim to represent every shade of political opinion.

Internal Party Democracy. The Lortie commission found that the established parties are held in low public esteem and are actively supported by no more than 2 per cent of Canadians; fail to attract activists from the environmental movement, the feminist movement, and many other special interest groups; turn people off with their particular brand of parliamentary squabbling; hog public political subsidies for themselves to the exclusion of smaller parties; spend their $2.6 million in annual research grants on electioneering instead of policy development; exercise little central control over the recruitment of political candidates; have little ability to mobilize members; have few rules of ethical conduct; and often fail to enforce even those.[4]

Yet, although they still act like private organizations, for the past 20 years the major political parties have been heavily subsidized from the public purse. The tax money reaches party coffers in the form of individual and corporate donations subsidized by income tax credits and also by direct partial reimbursement of election expenses. In addition the parties get large dollops of legally-mandated free broadcast time. Even the expenses of candidates for party leadership are now absorbed in substantial measure by the taxpayer through creative intra-party transfers of funds to take advantage of the political tax credit. The common-law marriage of private control with public funds is no longer acceptable, Lortie concluded, and should be replaced by legally sanctified party constitutional practices and membership requirements plus full financial disclosure and transparency rules:

> There are two broad reasons why the conduct of parties generates legitimate public concern. First...many interveners at our public hearings argued that, given the significant public subsidy of parties and their candidates, there is a public interest in ensuring that parties conduct their nomination and leadership processes in ways that meet the norms and expectations concerning use of public monies. Second... parties have a critical public role: they provide the vehicle

---

4   Royal Commission on Electoral Reform and Party Financing, Vol. 1, pp. 219-238

for nominating candidates and for choosing leaders, even prime ministers.... Because parties serve as the principal gatekeepers in determining which candidates and leaders are selected, there is a legitimate public interest in ensuring that fair and equitable procedures apply to the selection processes.[5]

The parties' inconsistency in the application of internal rules; their inability to rectify abuses when they do occur; their lack of reliable appeal procedures; and the extra weight assigned to privileged categories of members at leadership conventions all should be rectified by legally prescribed and enforceable constitutions for parties and their constituency associations, said Lortie, with the whole arrangement supervised by a new Canada Elections Commission.[6] If that is done, Lortie said, the election spending limits for registered parties should be raised to 70 cents per voter, about $12 million, and for local candidates to $50,000 plus 50 cents for every constituent in excess of 30,000. He proposed that taxpayers support the campaigns of both party leadership candidates and candidates for local riding nominations by making private donations to them eligible for political tax credits.[7]

---

5   Ibid. p. 245
6   Ibid. p. 247. Lortie recommends that this body be composed of political appointees, and the House of Commons has responded enthusiastically to this version of self-regulation. Most Canadians will want a more independent, judicial quality in any such oversight body. When politicians regulate politicians, as in the Ontario Election Commission, the temptations of mutual backscratching often prove overwhelming. In a recent decision, for example, Liberals and Conservatives on the Ontario commission voted against registering an organization called the Direct Democracy Party. The New Democratic Party objected that the name was too much like its own and the others actually bought the argument.
7   The royal commission ignored a suggestion by Mike Harris, leader of the Ontario Progressive Conservative Party, that political tax credits be made refundable. Harris, who introduced a private member's bill on the subject, said that the tax credit works only for Canadians who pay income tax and constitutes political discrimination against the poor, many of whom are working women. Canadians too poor to pay tax should get a refund from the government when they contribute to political parties, Harris argued.

To combat the embarrassing methods of politicians like Brian Mulroney and Joe Clark who recruited the votes of teeny-boppers and busloads of winos in their battles for political leadership, Lortie said only party members in good standing for at least 30 days should be allowed to vote for delegates to leadership conventions. No leadership candidate should spend more than 15 per cent of a party's election expense limit, about $2 million for a national party, on a personal quest for office. To forestall the widespread impression that leadership candidates are owned by anonymous benefactors, Lortie said the source of every gift of $250 or more should be identified and a preliminary public disclosure should be made the day before a leadership convention vote.

To round out the regulatory framework, Lortie said all constituency nominations should be decided at open conventions and no candidate for a nomination should spend more than 10 per cent of the riding's election expense limit — a ceiling, for example, of $6,500 in a riding with 60,000 voters.

Party Finance. The Liberals, Conservatives and New Democrats together collect an average of about $18 million a year in public assistance. Most of it takes the form of private donations financed by tax credits but in 1988, the last election year, the parties in addition received $18.6 million in direct payments from the public purse — $5 million to the three major national parties and $13.6 million to candidates, almost exclusively those of the major parties.

The system of direct payments to parties and candidates is a reward for election spending. The party head offices get back 22.5 per cent of their total election spending, provided only that they exceed 10 per cent of their spending limit. Riding candidates get back 50 per cent of their expenses to a maximum of 50 per cent of the riding spending limit, provided that they win at least 15 per cent of the popular vote. Said Lortie of all these arrangements, which date back to 1974:

At the heart of this reimbursement system lies the belief that candidates and parties perform important and necessary functions during elections in a democratic system; it is therefore in the public interest for the state to provide public funds to support these functions. Reimbursement also lessens candidates' and parties' reliance on large donations from a few donors and helps ensure that candidates and parties are able to conduct effective campaigns. Finally, reimbursement lowers the cost of running for office, thereby facilitating access to the system.[8]

He did not approve of rewarding spending, however, and instead proposed a subsidy system based on payments in proportion to votes received.

Communications Monopoly and Gag Laws. The official purpose of the entire system of regulating election expenses and election broadcasting is to create fair competition in elections. The system's balance is upset, Lortie said, if outsiders — unions, corporations or other groups not subject to regulation such as the National Citizens Coalition or the Pro-Canada Network — are allowed to mount television, radio and newspaper advertising campaigns which support or undermine any of the political parties during an election period.

Should such activity become widespread the purpose of the legislation would be destroyed, the reasonable opportunity it seeks to establish would vanish, and the overall goal of restricting the role of money in unfairly influencing election outcomes would be defeated.[9]

By way of illustrating the point, Lortie notes that in 1988 the candidacy of Democrat Michael Dukakis for the U.S. presidency was torpedoed by television ads suggesting that Dukakis, as governor of Massachussetts, was responsible for the actions of Willie Horton, a black felon who escaped while on prison leave and brutally raped a Maryland woman. The ads, financed by a purported-

---

8   Ibid. p. 364
9   Ibid. p. 327

ly independent group called Americans for Bush, were not considered part of the official campaign of Republican party candidate George Bush.

In Canada individuals, corporations, labor unions and other groups spent about $4.7 million on independent advertising during the 1988 election campaign.

> The vast proportion of independent expenditures was directed at the issue of free trade. Moreover, four times as much money was spent to promote free trade as was spent to oppose it.... The lopsided nature of the independent campaign raised a new question about the relationship between independent expenditures on issues and candidate and party spending limits.... Groups and individuals promoting free trade spent $0.77 on advertisements for every $1 of the entire advertising budget of the Progressive Conservative Party, whereas independent expenditures on advertisements against free trade accounted for only $0.13 for each $1 of the total advertising budgets of the two large parties opposing free trade.[10]

The implication, Lortie said, is that so-called independent issue advertising can easily be created to benefit one political party or hurt another and thus cannot and should not be distinguished from party election spending. He went on to suggest a limit of $1,000 on election spending by individuals or groups other than political parties — in effect a ban on television political advertising during campaigns by any entity other than a political party.

> It would be unfair, as well as unconstitutional, to ban all independent election spending.... [However] Canadian and comparative experience also demonstrate that any attempt to distinguish between partisan advocacy and issue advocacy — to prohibit spending on the former and to allow unregulated spending on the latter — cannot be sustained.[11]

---

10   Ibid. p. 338
11   Ibid. p. 340

An Alberta court in 1984 used the Charter of Rights and Freedoms to rule against Parliament's attempt to prevent groups from advertising directly for or against a political party. This year another Alberta judge, again in response to an application by David Sommerville and the National Citizens' Coalition, has again ruled against restrictions on groups other than political parties. Ignoring Lortie's argument about the futility of the distinction the House of Commons this spring passed a law preventing any group from spending more than $1,000 on direct political advertising naming candidates or parties but did not attempt to prevent indirect or issue advertising. Sommerville fought the gag law, arguing that "people vote for parties, not for issues." The Alberta court of Queen's Bench rejected Parliament's whole approach, finding that it offended three charter rights: freedom of expression, freedom of association, and the right to an informed vote. The Conservative government asked for a stay of the decision, but Canada's chief electoral officer, Jean-Pierre Kingsley, pre-empted the question by declaring that he will not enforce the law anywhere in Canada until all appeals have been completed. The effect is that there will be no restraint on independent advertising in the 1993 campaign and, as Lortie warned, that puts Canada's system of election expense limits in jeopardy. We'll propose a solution in Chapter Six in the context of a discussion of political broadcasting.

Brain Transplants for Political Parties. Lortie worried about another aspect of political life which has had far-reaching consequences for Canada — the near-total failure of the established parties to undertake long-term policy development or public political education. "Overall," he said, "Canadian political parties have a reputation for being weak other than in the performance of electoral functions" — a polite way of saying they know how to get elected but don't have a clue what to do when they get there.[12] His

---

12   Ibid. p. 295

proposed solution was to pump more taxpayer funding into party research foundations — 25 cents per vote for any party getting more than 5 per cent of the popular vote or about $1.5 million a year for the Conservatives, $900,000 for the Liberals and $600,000 for the NDP based on the 1988 vote distribution.

Succor for Small and Emerging Parties. Lortie had a small crisis of conscience, or perhaps an intuition about future court rulings, over the obstacles to small and new parties in the Canadian election system. There is an important connection, he said, between the attitudes which lead most Canadians to avoid any direct involvement with the established parties and the attitudes which lead some Canadians to vote, election after election, for parties which have no hope of putting a representative in the House of Commons. A democracy, he concluded, should show greater respect for those who don't think the established parties represent them.

Canada's laws for registering and financing political parties are stacked against small parties and new parties, Lortie acknowledged. The standard for official recognition — the nomination of candidates in at least 50 ridings at latest 28 days before a federal election — is tied to the electoral cycle in a way that confers a great advantage to established parties:

> The process does not allow the registration of emerging parties [Reform prior to 1988, for example, and the Bloc Québécois and the National Party since then] that acquire substantial public support between elections. This denies them access to the tax credit and to other public benefits available to registered parties. Allowing new parties to register between elections would promote fairness and accessibility and demonstrate that the electoral process and political process are open to parties [that differ] from the existing parties.[13]

Lortie said new parties should be allowed to register by petition on the signature of 5,000 supporters and all groups which

---

13   Ibid. p. 248

nominate at least 15 candidates should be allowed to place their party's name on the ballot. He also urged a change in political financing rules now designed to deny public funds to small parties.

> The requirement that parties must spend 10 per cent of their spending limit ignores a party's level of popular support entirely. It rewards only the well-financed parties. This has implications for the legitimacy of public funding rules.[14]

That spending threshold — 10 per cent for a national party and, after a recent change to the law, 30 per cent for a local candidate — and the stiff 15 per cent vote requirement to qualify for riding-level reimbursement to candidates "send a clear message to the smaller parties and their candidates as well as to independent candidates: their participation is not welcome." As Lortie realized, the established parties have been using their control of the Canada Elections Act to try to freeze the Canadian party system in its present form and in pursuit of that goal are deliberately violating the Charter of Rights and Freedoms. In the past, when new parties like Social Credit, the CCF or the Bloc Populaire appeared to shake up the complacency of the Liberals and Conservatives they did it without tax funding — but the established parties in those days didn't have big television advertising budgets financed from the public purse.

"In short," Lortie observed, "the present reimbursement system has disproportionately overcompensated the three largest parties and their candidates and undercompensated the smaller parties, their candidates, and independent candidates." He said a subsidy system based on electoral support and not the ability to spend money "would lead to a fairer distribution of public funding...and give emerging parties a fair opportunity to grow." He proposed a scheme in which national parties would receive 60 cents for each

---

14   Ibid. p. 364

vote and the local candidates $1 for each vote, with the payments to any party or candidate achieving 1 per cent of the vote or more.

"In European countries," commented Lortie, "vote-based public funding and low threshholds have contributed to a greater flexibility within the electoral system. The existing parties have not used their position of strength to block innovators. Instead the parties have ensured that equality of opportunity is part of the regulatory package."

The equality of opportunity Lortie proposes here is not the one generally available in Europe and the one that really matters — the opportunity to send representatives to the legislature in proportion to votes received. It is a minor consolation prize worth, on the basis of 1988 voting patterns, a modest $300,000 to all the parties outside Parliament combined. Sadly, some of the small parties are so accustomed to being kicked around that they were grateful for even that tiny consideration.

In fact, as Lortie knew full well, the barriers to public financing of small parties must end because they are unconstitutional. A judge of the Quebec Superior Court used the Charter of Rights and Freedoms in mid-1992, shortly after the Lortie report was completed, to strike down Ottawa's rule that candidates can't be reimbursed for election expenses unless they get 15 per cent of the vote.

> The right to vote includes the corollary right to be able to vote in an informed and rational manner after the citizen has had an opportunity to know the political options and programs supported by the candidates. It follows that the right to stand for election includes the right to be given an opportunity to communicate in an effective manner with the electorate in order to inform prospective voters of the issues and the position the candidate takes with respect to them. To require citizens to vote without being given a fair chance to know and understand the choices available to them is to effectively deny them their right to vote.... The evidence shows that effective communication...involves expense. In theory each candidate should be afforded an equal opportunity to communicate his views to the electorate; otherwise there is a distorted or incomplete view

of the issues. Of course perfect equality is impossible...but the law should not contribute to or aggravate inequalities.[15]

The Conservative government appealed that ruling in May, 1993, and by mid-August the appeal decision had not yet been rendered.

Candidate Selection. Long sections of the Lortie report are devoted to Charter-inspired handwringing about the failure of Canada's publicly-funded political parties to nominate women, members of visible minorities, and aboriginals in winnable ridings and get them elected to Parliament. This is a topic that Lortie had to approach gingerly because the name of the political game is winning seats, and it is not self-evident that such candidates will always give a party its best chance of winning in first-past-the-post elections. Here's how he tackled it:

Many of the problems associated with the nomination process — the low number of women recruited, for example — stem not from the high level of competition in a limited number of constituencies but from the large number of uncompetitive, relatively closed nomination contests conducted by local party insiders.... There is no public regulation of these processes...and little in the way of national or provincial party control.... While this decentralization stems from a longstanding tradition of localism in party affairs and is frequently praised in those terms, the structure and its results have raised a number of concerns [about]...the openness of the system. Close to two-thirds of constituency nomination contests are uncompetitive — that is, the nomination is by acclamation.... It is often assumed that this is the result of decisions by local executives. Opportunities exist to introduce changes to the selection process that will make it more open, more amenable to grassroots participation and more consistent with democratic principles.[16]

---

15   Gomery, J.S.C. of the Quebec Superior Court in Barrette and Payette vs. A.G. Canada, August 1992.
16   Lortie et al, op. cit. p. 265

PARLIAMENT LAUGHS AT LORTIE

This spring, knowing that a federal election could be avoided no longer, the Special Commons Committee on Electoral Reform chaired by Jim Hawkes (PC-Calgary West) finally went to work on the tricky parts of Lortie's year-old report.[17] In classic cherrypicking style the MPs took a bit of the report as intended, perverted other parts, and left large chunks on the shelf.

Candidates for Parliament used to pay a $200 election deposit which Lortie said served no valid public purpose. Hawkes' group of Liberals, Conservatives and New Democrats put forward a bill which raised the deposit for the upcoming 1993 election to $1,000. Ignoring the Quebec court ruling, they specified that $500 will be forfeited by candidates who don't get 15 per cent of the vote. Conservative House Leader Harvie Andre explained that the small parties are a nuisance and should be weeded out. Chris Lea, leader of the Green Party, was incensed: "We are already penalized into insignificance by the first-past-the-post voting system," he said. "These new fees represent a real threat to our continued legal existence and will drain money that could be better spent on research and education. This bastardization of the Lortie commission shows the ethical bankruptcy of this Parliament, and I am disgusted."

The House of Commons animus against small parties was so great that Bill C-114, while providing for the deregistration of parties which fail to nominate 50 candidates, indulged in some remarkable legal overkill. By law, deregistered parties are now forbidden to register again. They must liquidate all assets including printing presses, pay their bills, and turn over all remaining financial surpluses to the crown — even if the surpluses exceed public

---

17   The other members of the committee were Peter Milliken (Lib-Kingston and the Islands), Rod Murphy (NDP-Churchill), Patrick Boyer (PC-Etobicoke-Lakeshore), Geoff Wilson (PC-Swift Current-Maple Creek-Assiniboia), Michel Champagne (PC-Champlain), Charles-Eugene Marin (PC-Gaspé) and Pat Sobeski (PC-Cambridge).

funding received via the political tax credit. This rather drastic expropriation provision and the ban on party revival was likely to be contested in the courts by the Communist Party of Canada.

In a second bill which did not become law before Parliament adjourned, the Hawkes committee gave further evidence of three-party disdain for the Lortie commission. Instead of Lortie's proposal for a spending limit of $0.70 per voter, the MPs proposed $1.20. On the revenue side, they reached for an increase of 11 per cent in the rate of public dole to selected political parties — those which spend more than 10 per cent of their election limit. The committee also ignored Lortie's proposals for equitable sharing of election broadcast opportunties and proposed a division which would prevent the three new political parties with some financial clout — Reform, the National Party and the Bloc Québécois — from buying significant television time.

The committee liked one of Lortie's ideas a lot. It attempted to launch the Canada Elections Commission, a body to be chosen by politicians to replace the RCMP as the authority responsible for investigating and prosecuting all election irregularities. The new body would have the authority to make voluntary compliance deals with the accused Members of Parliament, and that part of the royal commission package seemed to suit the MPs just fine.

"The electoral process lies at the heart of our democracy and Canadians have a right to the best law that our human ingenuity can devise to serve them," said Hawkes in summing up his committee's handiwork. The rest of the royal commission's recommendations, he indicated, would have to be considered by somebody else — perhaps in time for the 1998 federal election.

LESSONS FROM THE LORTIE COMMISSION

Parliament has made clear that it is not interested in either thorough-going party reform as proposed by Lortie or the kind of party shakeup and political realignment that would flow from proportional representation. The three parties which now monopolize Parliament are interested only in muddling along and so the impetus for real changes, if we are to have any, must come from outside Parliament. That will require, as we said in Chapter One, a popular movement or a coalition of interest groups acting in concert to bring the necessary pressures to bear. Before leaving the wreckage of the Lortie commission report, however, we should make some further use of it. Real democrats who want to shake up the party system will find help in some of the insights the commission gained into the operation of our major political parties.

THE PARTY SYSTEM'S SHAKY FOUNDATIONS

Lortie's attempts to make the royal commission research team think positive thoughts about Canada's political parties and voting system were not entirely successful. Professors R.K. Carty of UBC and Lynda Erikson of Simon Fraser University, for example, provided a lengthy portrait which suggests that the major national parties have extremely shallow roots in society and almost no control over their central activity: choosing and labelling candidates for the ballot.

> No matter what else it may or may not do, by nominating 50 candidates to contest a general election under a common label any organization is entitled to be registered as a party. It is through this process of labelling candidates that parties come to make their principal contribution to the conduct of electoral democracy and responsible government as it is practised in Canada. One might expect that a process so central...would be carefully regulated by the Canada Elections Act...but such is not the case. The process is treated as if it were the *ad hoc* business of small groups of autonomous electors.[18]

The completely unregulated nature of the nominating process is surprising, given the extent of state funding of political parties and the fact that, in some situations, a party nomination is tantamount to election to Parliament. The impression now exists, the re-

---

18 Carty, R.K. and Erickson, Lynda. Candidate Nomination in Canada's National Political Parties, RC Research Studies, Vol. 13, p. 97

searchers say, that "organized groups are routinely able to penetrate local party associations and buy a nomination" and therefore often a seat in the House of Commons.

One dramatic upset occurred in Edmonton during the 1984 general election when Marcel Lambert, a 27-year Parliamentary veteran, former cabinet minister and Speaker of the House, was out-manoeuvred in a long four-ballot nomination by a 30-year old rival at a meeting attended by a thousand local activists.[19]

The Canada Elections Act gives a party leader the power to withhold the party label from a nominee and in that way exercise a veto power over candidate selection, but some party insiders have come to believe that further regulation is needed. Liberal MP Albina Guarnieri told the royal commission that nearly 10 per cent of the members of her Mississauga East riding association were also Conservative party members and constituted almost a quarter of the local Conservative association. This cross-membership phenomenon, she suggested, deprives committed one-party members of control over who their candidate will be.

At the same time, however, surveys of Liberal and Conservative convention delegates show that strong majorities in both parties think the central party apparatus and leader should be compelled to accept the choice of a local nominating meeting.[20] These advocates of local sovereignty have been giving Liberal leader Jean Chrétien considerable flak this spring over his attempts to pre-select potential cabinet talent such as former Toronto mayor Art Eggleton and Metro Housing chair Jean Augustine and parachute his national party choices into safe ridings.

The research also found these general practices in the riding associations: nomination meetings are under the control of the local executive and are called when it sees fit; a certain proportion of out-of-riding membership is usually permitted, although in the

---

19   Ibid. p. 102
20   Ibid. p. 105

Conservative party it is constitutionally forbidden; the waiting period between joining a party and voting is usually one or two weeks; the central party apparatus is seldom involved in the candidate search; and the result of a nomination meeting is almost always definitive. Only six per cent of the nominations were appealed and most of the original decisions were upheld. "The basic message of the data is that Canadian parties require very little commitment from individuals in exchange for the right to vote at nomination meetings," the researchers concluded. "It makes the parties open and vulnerable to outside interests. At the same time it might well prove difficult to regulate associations whose membership is so fluid and unevenly institutionalized."[21]

Table 2.1

Membership Requirements
of Nomination Meeting Participants
(percentage of constituency associations)

	Liberal	PC	NDP
One week or less	25	46	15
8-15 days	17	28	13
16-30 days	38	23	45
30 days or more	21	3	28
Total	100	100	100

21   Ibid. p. 112

The final dimension of this portrait of the grassroots of the Canadian party system is to look at the size of riding association memberships and the turnout at nomination meetings.

[The data] reveal fairly low levels of participation. The average constituency has nearly 60,000 electors while the typical (median) constituency association has but 532 members: 44 per cent of the constituency parties in the country have fewer than 500 members; just under one third have 1,000 or more. The figures on the nomination meeting, arguably the most important decision taken, support the portrait of limited party involvement. On average only about one third of a riding's membership attends.... This makes the candidate selection process one in which those citizens who do participate see that they are having an influence. This also makes it one that can be manipulated with relatively few resources.[22]

The researchers note that there is a serious contradiction at the heart of the Canadian party system. "Parties exist to nominate candidates under a common label, to impose common obligations on mainly local candidates in exchange for the promise of nationwide political success." Yet the candidate selection is controlled by tiny groups steeped in a tradition, almost a religion, of local control. It's hard to know whether to view it as "a national process in local clothing or a parochial event parading under a national label."[23]

Nominating meetings where parties have some chance of victory are likely to be held well in advance of an election at the convenience of the incumbent MP or the local party clique. While contested nominations attended by hundreds or even thousands of "instant" Liberals or Conservatives attract media attention, they are rare. In 1988 only 15 per cent of all riding associations had a nomination contest involving three or more contestants and only half of those required more than one ballot to determine a winner. Riding membership increases when incumbents must recruit sup-

22   Ibid. p. 115
23   Ibid. p. 171

Table 2.2
Participation in Nomination Meetings

Association Membership Size	Percentage of Associations
0-100	11
101-499	33
500-1000	24
1001+	31
Total	100
Mean	975 members
Median	532 members

Nomination meeting turnout

Percentage of Membership	Percentage of Associations
Less than 20	28
20-36	23
37-54	25
More than 54	24
Total	100
Mean	39
Median	36

Source: Carty and Erikson, RC Research Vol.13.

porters to beat off challengers who have also recruited new party members, but even in those unusual battles the riding association membership rises to an average of only 2,700. Although a few candidates have spent $30,000 or more in nomination contests, the average cost of a party nomination in Canada is $1,400 and the median cost is $100. Almost 90 per cent of incumbent MPs who want to stand again are unopposed. Incumbent MPs and hopeless situations together account for about one-third of all nominating situations, but in 1988 two thirds of all nominations were by acclamation. Almost half the available desirable nominations were decided by acclamation.

> The average membership in uncontested associations with no incumbent was just 500. Even accepting that many of those nominations are not particularly desirable in that they represent normally unwinnable seats, simple arithmetic suggests that winning many of these nominations would require rather little. That being so, the fact that so few are contested indicates what low levels of competition characterize Canadian party life.... Even in contested nominations for open seats turnout still averages less than 50 per cent [of riding association membership].[24]

There are "significant numbers of potentially easy access points (uncontested good nominations) available for individuals wanting into the system, although most of them are on the opposition side of the party system," the researchers concluded. They also noted that, despite declarations by national party officials that they want more women and members of visible minorities as candidates, there was little evidence in 1988 of a concerted effort to bring that about.

> Under the guise of tradition and the rationale of local autonomy, the national political parties...have largely abdicated any significant role in the nomination of their candidates. It is then misleading to argue that Canadian political parties as national institutions are responsible for recruiting men and women into political life. They hardly even act as gatekeepers to the system. More typically they

---

24   Ibid. p. 125

exist as rather general electoral syndicates that lend their name to activities of local groups.... The very lack of standard rules and the permeability of the process may create a veil of ignorance about it that intimidates and excludes outsiders.[25]

The result of the local selection process is "a House of Commons full of middle-aged, middle-class, well-educated males because they are the ones the three national parties largely nominate in the constituencies in which they have much prospect of electing a member." The most significant change in recent years has been a sharp drop in the number of lawyer candidates to only 11 per cent of the total, and a decline in the political experience of candidates. One quarter of all nominees in 1988 had belonged to their party four years or less.

These are hardly men and women well schooled in the party and its traditions. They are conscripts who cannot realistically be expected to play an active and independent role in party affairs. But, given that the wider party has so small a role in their recruitment, it can hardly expect more. At the same time, local associations that send individuals with such weak party roots to Ottawa can hardly expect them to stand up to the caucus leadership in any systematic fashion.[26]

The commission's evidence on atrophy at the party roots is consistent with the portrait of opportunistic brokerage parties and disenchanted voters which emerged in Chapter One. There is no reason why large numbers of Canadians could or should feel strong loyalty to political parties which themselves don't exhibit any strong commitment to interests or ideas. Pierre Lortie and the other royal commissioners, all top party insiders, made preserving, refining and ploughing more public funds into these shaky political structures their mission and the substance of their report. Political outsiders — the 98 per cent of us who have no attach-

25   Ibid. p. 176
26   Ibid. p. 178

ment to the present party system other than voting — deserved better from them. The country is suffering an ongoing crisis of democratic leadership which must be addressed through democratic political parties. For $20 million the royal commission owed us a serious examination of the voting system which could give us what we need — a real change in the way our political parties and leaders behave. They didn't do it, so we'll have to do it ourselves.

3

FAIR VOTING: PROPORTIONAL REPRESENTATION

A class may have a great number of votes
in every constituency in the kingdom
and not obtain a single representative in this House.
Their right of voting may be only
the right of being outvoted.

— John Stuart Mill
to the British House of Commons, 1866

The only two headlines I really liked?
"Mulroney Wins Big Majority"
and the second one that said
"Mulroney Re-elected With Big Majority,"
because you know what?
All the other stuff doesn't really matter.

— Brian Mulroney, June 1993

A leader must do more than
see unpopular policies through a legislature.
A leader must make unpopular policies popular.

— William Thorsell, Editor,
The Globe and Mail, June 1993

CANADA'S DEMOCRACY GAP cannot be closed until we put aside the rules of electoral competition we now use and substitute a voting system based on proportional representation.

British voting rules are inherently unfair and, as we described in Chapter One, often produce extreme distortions in representation. In a two-party rivalry, for example, a party which attracts just one more vote than its rival in each constituency can win every seat in a legislature and leave 49.9 per cent of the electorate without representation. The potential distortions become even more severe when more parties are competing. Proportional representation, by contrast, guarantees the equal influence of each voter by assigning seats in the legislature to political parties in proportion to their share of the total vote cast.

Proportional representation or PR voting systems, widely employed in Europe, assume as we do that political parties are essential to the conduct of modern democratic government. The Europeans, however, give the highest priority to accurate representation of voter support for political parties because there is no better measure of a democratic people's ideas about how it wants to be governed. Most parliamentary democracies other than the United Kingdom, Australia, New Zealand and France have already accepted this approach to representation and Canadian democracy will benefit from accepting it too.

Even the report of the Lortie royal commission, although preprogrammed to reject proportional representation, is littered with language and analysis which contradicts its endorsement of British voting rules. "At the heart of the electoral process lies the principle of the equality of voters," Lortie proclaimed at one reckless moment.[1] At another point he suggested that citizens ought to have "an equal opportunity to exercise meaningful influence over

---

1   Lortie et al, op. cit., p. 325

the outcome of elections," and that "for this equality of opportunity to be realized in the electoral process, our electoral laws must also be fair... The federal electoral process must first and foremost reflect and promote fairness."[2] In discussing the allocation of seats in the House of Commons to provinces he said: "Equality of the vote is secured if the assignment of seats to provinces conforms to the principle of proportionate representation and if the drawing of the constituency boundaries conforms to the principle of representation by population."[3] In deciding how political parties should be assisted financially, he proposed public funding in proportion to popular vote. In dealing with the out-of-country vote he proposed that citizens who didn't know the names of candidates in their home ridings be allowed simply to vote for the political parties. Finally, when Lortie confronted the question of parliamentary representation for Canada's widely-dispersed aboriginal peoples, he found it could be resolved only by a form of proportional representation. He recommended special aboriginal constituencies and special voluntary aboriginal voting registers to make possible the accumulation of aboriginal votes. "They should be directly represented in Parliament in order to participate in statutory changes that affect them," the report said. Here's how it justified the flip-flop on proportional representation:

> We recommend the continuation of the Canadian system of single-member constituencies defined in a geographic manner because we consider it the best way to achieve the desired equality and efficacy of the vote within the Canadian system of responsible parliamentary government generally. We recognize, nonetheless, that there is nothing "natural" or sacrosanct about this approach. In accepting an exception...(we) acknowledge the crucial fact that although Aboriginal people constitute a minority of the population in every

---

2   Ibid. p. 321
3   Ibid. p. 133

province, the total number of Aboriginal people in Canada...is larger than the total population of each of the four Atlantic provinces.[4]

We think most Canadians will agree that the exception should be the rule. Aboriginals and all other Canadians who choose to associate politically should have equal opportunity to be represented in Parliament in proportion to their numbers. British voting rules make that impossible, and proportional representation rules will make it normal. In the case of aboriginals, for example, there is no need for apartheid constituencies and apartheid voting registers. Ovide Mercredi and the other aboriginal leaders will simply register the First Nations Party of Canada, aboriginal Canadians wherever they are will vote for it if they want to, and its leaders will be sent to Parliament along with the leaders of every other political grouping with significant popular support.

The basic question — whether to keep the British voting rules or switch to a reformed voting system based on proportional representation — must be put to the Canadian people in a national referendum. To get that referendum we will need an active citizens' movement which we will call here, for purposes of discussion, the Democracy League.

The most probable effects of a switch in voting rules have already been described: a reduction in size and change in character of our established parties and an increase in the number and diversity of parties represented in Parliament. The result of that would almost certainly be the end of single-party government but, where that might once have been perceived as a problem, most Canadians would now see it as an advantage. Our single-party governments may have no grand design — Pierre Trudeau's come to mind — but when like the Mulroney Conservatives they get an idea or two they are far too inclined, as the editor of *The Globe and Mail* has observed, to push them through Parliament and into law without a public mandate and without building a public consensus. We Canadians are by no means alone in our concerns about a

---

4   Ibid. p. 182

malfunctioning democracy. Citizens of both the United Kingdom and New Zealand have realized in recent years that the old British voting rules are standing in the way of the kind of Parliament and the style of government they want.

THE MOTHER OF PARLIAMENTS

In the United Kingdom, where parties actually put forward serious election programs and live by them, discontent with the country's polarized two-party politics and the tendency of British voting rules to perpetuate it recurs with great regularity but has never resulted in electoral reform. The established Labour and Conservative parties fight to keep the rules in place while reformers, even during the one interlude 60 years ago when they had the upper hand, have failed to agree on which new system to adopt. The issue of voting rules surfaced strongly again a decade ago when a major split in the Labour party created an opening for a new centrist formation, the Liberal/Social Democratic Alliance. Britain's voters responded enthusiastically, giving the Alliance 25 per cent of the vote in 1983. The British voting rules, however, gave the Alliance a tiny and disappointing 3.5 per cent share of the House of Commons while Labour and the Conservatives maintained their staunch alliance against electoral reform. Liberal/SDP support has since declined and with it so have prospects for subtler alternatives to the U.K.'s rocky lurches between Labour and Tory government. Throughout the 1980s the U.K. majority goverments led by radical Conservative Prime Minister Margaret Thatcher were not particularly popular. They operated on the support of just 42 per cent of the electorate.

NEW ZEALAND REFERENDUM

In New Zealand, a sister parliamentary democracy, citizens will decide by referendum later this year whether to switch to proportional representation. In a preliminary plebiscite in September 1992 a whopping 85 per cent of New Zealand voters rejected the traditional British voting rules. Both major parties in New

Zealand, Labour and the governing National Party, are strongly opposed to the impending reform but the electorate is now poised to overrule its political elite on this fundamental democratic issue.

The path to voting reform has been a twisted one. In the mid-1980s the governing Labour Party appointed a royal commission on electoral reform to reconsider the issue of effective representation for New Zealand's aboriginals, the Maori, and to address the long-standing frustrations of supporters of New Zealand's smaller parties. Social Credit had recently won 21 per cent of the popular vote and received only 2 per cent of the seats in the House of Representatives. The electoral reform commission in 1986 recommended a system of modified proportional representation which offered hope to third-party voters and a flexible mechanism for Maori representation. Labour Prime Minister David Lange, holding office with an inflated parliamentary majority, didn't like the plan and stalled by promising a referendum on the matter after the 1987 general election. The Labour party raked in much of the small party vote, boosted its parliamentary majority, and then repudiated the referendum promise.

National Party leader Jim Bolger stepped into the gap, promising a referendum on voting reform if he became prime minister. He formed a government in 1990 and, although no fan of proportional representation, kept his word with the preliminary plebiscite last September. As the final referendum draws nearer most Labour and National party politicians, business groups and newspaper and broadcast outlets in New Zealand are campaigning hard against the proposed change. The question remains open but, after years of deception, that country's electors finally have voting reform within their grasp.

THE WESTMINSTER FACTOR

In all these Commonwealth democracies, despite their social differences, the voters have common complaints about the style of Parliamentary government. A background paper for the Lortie commission summed it up this way:

In the Westminister model, while the government may be responsible to the assembly, system dynamics and party discipline ensure that individual deputies are constrained in their behavior and have little policy influence. Parliament itself is primarily a law-passing rather than a law-making body since the cabinet sets public policy. The focus increasingly is on the personalities of the prime minister and the leader of the opposition rather than on party policies *per se*. The prime minister is a dominant figure, and indeed the power of the executive is extensive and essentially unbridled.[5]

Elsewhere the same study summarizes the chief characteristics of the system as "two major parties which alternate in power, powerful prime minister, weak legislature, and a clear and formal opposition with little effective input in the policy process." In practice this means voters watching Parliament on television see members slanging back and forth during Question Period or bobbing up and down during roll call votes to rubber-stamp decisions by the party leaders, and not much more. We'd like to think that our well-paid, well-pensioned representatives study, debate and shape the laws that govern us but we've learned — especially since Prime Minister Pierre Trudeau so cruelly dismissed them as "nobodies" — that there isn't all that much more to the job of being a backbench or opposition MP than what we can see. Because many of them are talented people they are deeply frustrated by the severe limitations of the job, and some are honest enough to admit it.

Patrick Boyer (PC -Etobicoke Lakeshore), says the role of a backbench government Member of the Parliament of Canada "is like that of a Canadian soldier in the 1942 Dieppe Raid: fodder in an intended ambush to satisfy the larger workings of the system's grand design.... If you care strongly about trying to make things happen, frustration results and you conclude an MP really is a nobody."[6]

---

5   Chandler, W. and Siaroff, A. Parties and Party Government in Advanced Democracies, RC Research Vol. 13, p. 202

6   Boyer, P. *The People's Mandate*, 1992, p. 226

In Ottawa, politicians have been reacting to the decline in public esteem for Parliament by discussing the possible use of electronic voting cards, for example, so the television cameras won't catch them abasing themselves, again and again, in ritual roll call voting on party orders. A real change in parliamentary practices would be more to the point, but that requires a change in the relationships among the political parties and that in turn brings us back to electoral reform. As long as single-party majorities are the goal of party competition there's little room for a government to be seen bargaining or compromising with the opposition — or vice versa. The dynamic in Parliament and its committees changes drastically only when there's a minority government which must consult the opposition parties to avoid measures that will lead to its defeat. This weakening of prime ministerial authority doesn't necessarily paralyze a government. The Pearson Liberal administrations of 1963 and 1965 and the Trudeau government of 1972 were active and well regarded at the time and, cooperating with the NDP, passed substantial measures including the Canada Pension Plan, the Canada Assistance Plan, the guaranteed income supplement for old age pensions, universal medical care insurance, and the law establishing Petro-Canada.

The civilities between parties during a term of minority government are tactical and fleeting, however, and cannot offset the permanent temptation of easy electoral gain offered by the British voting rules. The government and opposition parties poll relentlessly, each looking for some small shift in public opinion which, on a sudden election gamble, might translate into a large shift in the makeup of Parliament and the big jackpot — an undeserved majority government. For a different model of parliamentary behavior we must look to Europe.

THE EUROPEAN EXAMPLE

Proportional representation is the principle shaping legislatures throughout Western Europe in democracies like Germany, Austria, Denmark, the Netherlands, Belgium, Sweden, Norway, Finland, Italy and Greece. Each of the PR countries uses slightly different electoral arrangements which create different wrinkles in the internal workings of each political system. The chief political characteristics of the European democracies are strong legislatures, influential legislative committees, and coalition governments.[7] The largest parties in the PR countries are not large enough to win a clear majority of the popular vote and so do not command a majority in the legislature. This does not lead, as it would here, to unstable legislatures forever on the brink of new elections. Instead elections are followed by bargaining between parties, often along lines signalled to the electorate in advance, to determine the composition and program of coalition governments.

There is a stronger focus in these countries on political parties and detailed political programs and less emphasis on the personalities of leaders, and the prime minister is not always the formal or most powerful leader of his party.

The basic patterns of government formation have varied considerably from long periods of one-party dominance or near dominance in Sweden (Social Democrats) and Italy (Christian Democrats) to shifting multi-party alliances to alternating two-party coalitions in Germany and Austria.

The political culture associated with proportional representation is less adversarial than Canada's. Instead of relying on an assertive parliamentary majority, European democracy tries to limit, divide, separate and share power in a variety of ways. It features corporatist policy making with a long-term outlook and a general intertwining of parliamentary politics with the bureaucracy and powerful interest groups.[8]

The proportional representation package offers a practical response to what has become an intractable problem for Canadians — the power of special interest groups such as the Business Council on National Issues which, due to Parliament's weakness, are able to exert most of their influence out of public view. Our desire to see public business done in open legislative

---

7   Chandler and Siaroff, op. cit., p. 201

8   Ibid.

committees where the interest groups face effective representatives of the people is not impractical, but simply European.

STABLE AND EFFECTIVE GOVERNMENT

Some critics of proportional representation argue that it must lead to unstable and ineffective government. There is much evidence to the contrary, but the favorite negative example is Italy whose unstable coalition governments and pervasive political corruption are attributed to the fragmenting effects of Italy's PR voting system. In the election of 1987, for example, no fewer than 14 parties won seats in the Italian Chamber of Deputies. This argument, however, places too heavy a responsibility on parties like the Lombard League, the Val d'Aosta Union, the South Tyrol People's Party and the Sardinian Action Party, which among them held 1 per cent of the seats in the legislature.

A more plausible explanation of Italy's political dilemma is its ideological divisions, the size of its Communist Party (now the Democratic Party of the Left) and the determination of other parties to exclude the Communists from government. In five elections up to 1987 the Communists were Italy's second-largest party, winning between 27 and 34 per cent of the vote. The Christian Democratic Party, oscillating between 33 and 39 per cent in popular support, continued to anchor every government as it has since the end of World War II. As the president of Fiat summed it up, the Christian Democrats controlled 80 per cent of the patronage with 40 per cent of the seats because there was no acceptable alternative to them.

The Italian people, prodded by former Christian Democrat politician Mario Segni, have now chosen an electoral reform path which promises to shake up the Italian party structure and bring an end to the long-standing parliamentary stalemate. Responding to a citizen referendum initiated by Segni's Democratic Alliance, Italians have voted to adopt a modified system of proportional representation which resembles the German electoral system. In elections to be held late this year three-quarters of the Chamber of Deputies will be elected from new single-member constituencies, while the remaining one-quarter will be selected from party lists in a way that brings the overall result as close as possible to proportional representation. Segni campaigned by arguing that the change would encourage a consolidation of parties on the left, provoke further changes within the Democratic Party of the Left, and finally make possible a government of the centre-left in Italy.

Prior to the mammoth bribery scandal and the disgrace of so many Christian Democratic politicians and corporate leaders this year it was not clear that Segni's scenario would prevail. The Democratic Party of the Left is dominant in the central regions around Florence, Perugia and Bologna but, despite significant strength elsewhere, would not likely have been able to win first-past-the-post elections in the north or south. Now, however, with the new voting rules favoring large parties and the Christian Democrats in a state of collapse, it is entirely possible that Italy's next government will be dominated by the Democratic Party of the Left. From a Canadian perspective it is instructive to watch both Italy and New Zealand, each trying to correct serious defects in its system of representation, converging on a system of modified proportional representation.

Taking a broader view of European representative democracy, we see that voter turnout — a useful measure of public attitudes — averages around 84 per cent in nine PR countries, about 10 per cent higher than the typical Canadian turnout for a federal election and close to the 90 per cent level reached in countries with compulsory voting. More than voters in Canada, voters in PR countries appear to believe their ballot matters.

A quality of life index indicates that the income distribution in the PR countries is somewhat less unequal than ours, and that they rate better on an index of democratic quality including factors for freedom of the press, free association, competitive party systems, strong parties and interest groups, and effective legislatures.[9]

---

9   The index was first prepared by U.S. political scientist Robert Dahl and published in his book *Polyarchy: Participation and Opposition*, 1971. Cited by Lijphart, A., Constitutional Choices for New Democracies, in Diamond and Plattner, *The Global Resurgence of Democracy*, 1992, p. 152

Critics of PR argue that one-party government produces firmer, more effective economic policy leadership than is possible in PR countries where executive power is shared among different parties.

The evidence is not conclusive but appears to point in the opposite direction. From 1961 to 1988 economic growth in the nine PR countries averaged 3.5 per cent yearly, the same as the average in Canada, the U.K., New Zealand, Australia and the U.S. The U.S. had the best record of price stability with inflation of 5.1 per cent. The PR countries were second-best at 6.3, and the Commonwealth four worst at 7.5 per cent. On the unemployment scale, the PR countries were markedly superior with average unemployment of 4.4 per cent compared with 6.1 in both the U.S. and the four Commonwealth countries.[10] A possible explanation is that good macroeconomic performance is the result of a steady hand on the levers of government rather than a strong one. Changes of government which result in dramatic shifts in economic policy are likely to impair economic performance, while PR systems are more likely to be consistently centrist in policy orientation. In economic policy quick decisions are not necessarily wise ones and policies supported by a broad consensus, although slower in the making, are more likely to be carried out successfully and to remain on course than policies imposed by a "strong" government against the wishes of important interest groups.

The point is perhaps best made by noting that Italy, for all the apparent messiness of its coalition-forming, had a better record of economic performance over nearly three decades than the United Kingdom despite the U.K.'s "strong" governments, and even though the Italians had no good luck comparable to the U.K.'s North Sea oil discoveries. "Multi-party and coalition governments seem to be messy, quarrelsome and inefficient in contrast to the clear authority of strong presidents and strong one-party cabinets, but we should not be deceived by these superficial appearances,"

---

10   Ibid. p. 154

says one U.S. authority. "The argument should not be about governmental aesthetics but about actual performance."[11]

PROPORTIONAL REPRESENTATION IN CANADA

Canadians have complained about the shortcomings of the voting system since shortly after Confederation without ever getting around to changing its essential features. During the first great voter rebellion against the two-party system Parliament in 1923 endorsed proportional representation "in principle" at the insistence of the Progressive Party. The Progressives were drawn one by one into the established parties, however, and the idea went no further. At the provincial level British Columbia (1952 and 1953), Alberta (1926 to 1959) and Manitoba (1920 to 1958) have used preferential ballots, and the latter two have used a transferable vote in city districts.[12] Alberta's experiments in voting reform ended when they proved helpful to opponents of the Social Credit government led by Ernest Manning, father of Reform Party leader Preston Manning.

More recently serious discussion of proportional representation has been confined to Quebec where a series of weird provincial election results for a time made reform a hot topic. In 1966 the Union Nationale stepped out of the political grave and formed a government despite winning only 41 per cent of the vote to 47 per cent for the Liberal party. Rene Levesque's Parti Quebecois revived the issue in 1973 after winning 30 per cent of the vote but only six seats against 102 for Robert Bourassa's Liberals. But three years later Levesque won a majority in the Quebec National Assembly with only 38 per cent of the vote and his enthusiasm for PR immediately waned. In subsequent years, although detailed reports were written, nobody bothered to change the law. The separatist PQ, like every other party that ever attained dominant status, was

11   Ibid. p. 157
12   Cassidy, M., Fairness and Stability in Canadian Elections: The Case for an Alternative Electoral System. 1992 manuscript.

seduced by the pleasures of easy majority power. The memory of those Quebec debates lingers, however, and gives the idea of voting reform through proportional representation even greater support among Quebec voters than it has in other parts of Canada.

During the late 1970s, with the Parti Quebecois holding office in Quebec, a federal Task Force on National Unity chaired by Jean-Luc Pepin and John Robarts expressed concern about the corrosive effects on public opinion of Quebec block voting and the frequent underrepresentation of Western Canada in the national government.

> The simple fact is that our elections produce a distorted image of the country, making provinces appear more unanimous in their support of one federal party or another than they really are.... In a country like Canada this sort of situation leads to a sense of alienation and exclusion from power.[13]

The Robarts-Pepin group recommended that 60 extra members of Parliament be added to the House of Commons, distributed in proportion to each party's popular vote and selected to shore up weaknesses in regional representation.

The Macdonald Royal Commission on the Economic Union, the group which reported in 1985 and sold Brian Mulroney on the "leap of faith" into free trade with the United States, was also tempted by proportional representation but not enough to endorse it wholeheartedly. The commission viewed the imbalances in party representation as a problem of appearances with effects on public opinion but little impact on the actual practice of Canadian government. Proportional representation would cure a cosmetic difficulty but at too high a price, the commission suggested, because it disliked the ongoing prospect of minority, two-party or multi-party governments. Instead, as a sop to sentiment in Western Canada, Donald Macdonald proposed proportional representation of parties in an elected but weakened Senate. Only if such a

---

13   Task Force on Canadian Unity, Vol. I, p. 105

Senate reform did not come to pass, he suggested, should proportional representation be applied to the House of Commons, and in that case he endorsed the Pepin-Robarts proposal for 60 additional members.[14,15]

The Lortie commission on electoral reform in 1991 said there were real advantages for Quebecers in always having large numbers of members on the government side and negative consequences for westerners for being so often underrepresented in government. But, Lortie said, the very fact that the House of Commons had taken no action on the Pepin-Robarts and Macdonald proposals effectively put an end to the matter. Lortie and company took the same escape hatch as Macdonald and urged Parliament to consider, instead of reform of the Commons, Senate reform.

ONE MAN'S INQUIRY

A member of the royal commission staff, former NDP MP Michael Cassidy, took up the forbidden investigation of proportional representation in a private study completed for the Donner Canadian Foundation in 1992. Close to 100 of the 900 submissions received by the royal commission advocated proportional representation, Cassidy reported, although most of these were from individuals "rather than from influential groups or political parties."

Cassidy tested Canada's voting system against principles of fair voting set out by the New Zealand electoral reform commission: all votes should be of equal value regardless of party chosen; voters should have a reasonable chance of being represented by someone of their political persuasion; the number of votes needed to elect a member should be relatively equal be-

---

14   Royal Commission on the Economic Union, 1985, Vol. III, p. 390, cited in Cassidy, op. cit., p. 5

15   The federal government proposed a Senate elected by proportional representation voting rules during constitutional negotiations in 1991, but provincial premiers didn't like it and the idea was dropped.

tween parties; a party's strength in Parliament should reflect the strength of its vote in the country; minor parties should have a reasonable chance to elect members; but access for minor parties should not go so far as to make the legislature ineffective. "Canada's electoral system falls far short of fairness on all criteria except the last," Cassidy concluded. "The values of equality and fairness associated with liberal democracy take second place in Canada to the objective of stable government."

The average variance between the leading party's proportion of the vote and its proportion of Commons seats in the past four elections was 16 percentage points, Cassidy calculated. The other parties experienced a corresponding 16 point shortfall. "As the 1988 election result [Mulroney's 43 per cent majority] indicated, this bias can be enough to lift a party to a clear majority of seats in the House of Commons once it achieves above 40 per cent of the vote."

The voting system's tendency to overamplify the vote of large parties in the past has benefited parties with 30 per cent of the vote or more and could benefit the Bloc Québécois in 1993, Cassidy foresaw. "If representation from the rest of Canada was dispersed among four or five parties it might be very hard to form an alliance that could command continuing support in the House of Commons," he wrote. "The plurality system, rather than being a source of stability, is beginning to contribute to instability in Canadian government."

WHAT KIND OF PROPORTIONAL REPRESENTATION?

Once we decide to reject British voting rules and replace them with proportional representation we'll still have to choose — as they did in New Zealand in a second question on the 1992 plebiscite — which of the several forms of PR we prefer. The basic variables are the magnitude of the constituency, the style of balloting, and the mathematical procedure for allocating seats among parties when the voting numbers don't work out evenly.

By far the most important of these in determining the fit between popular vote and allocation of seats is the magnitude of the constituency — the number of seats its voters control.[16] There is, as we know from more than 100 years of experience, no room for proportionality in single-member ridings. One party wins the seat and all the other voters and parties get nothing. Adding seats to the constituency increases the possibility of providing representation to supporters of second, third, and additional parties in proportion to voter numbers. One way to achieve near-complete proportionality between votes and seats and accomodate all political parties is to treat the entire country as a single electoral district. Under that arrangement, and with Canada's House of Commons at 295 members, a party with as little as 0.34 per cent of the national popular vote could claim a seat. Supporters of small parties find that proposition attractive and leaders of large parties don't. What the rest of us think can't be known definitively until the ballots from our proposed referendum are counted.

On the votes cast in the 1988 election a national PR system for Canada would have elected six members of the Reform Party, one from the Confederation of Regions, one Green and, believe it or not, one Rhinoceros. Two countries — The Netherlands and Israel, both of them physically small — conduct their elections with all the seats in a single pool and achieve a very high degree of proportionality in representation. The corollary, however, is that voters must choose between party lists rather than individual candidates. This in turn confers on the party leaders and central office a high degree of control over the selection of candidates, their placement on the party list, and their chances of being elected — the sort of control Liberal leader Jean Chrétien felt he needed this year to secure nominations and seats in Parliament for some of the star candidates around whom he hopes to build a cabinet.

We may prefer somewhat smaller electoral districts and, to a point, that can work well. One option is to use the regions as electoral districts — 89 seats in the West, 99 in Ontario, 75 in Quebec

---

16　An extensive mathematical analysis of electoral systems and discussion of the political implications of different arrangements is presented in Taagepera, R. and Shugart, M., *Seats and Votes*, 1989.

and 32 in the Atlantic. Those numbers are large enough to guarantee a high degree of proportionality in party representation. The large districts would accommodate a small but growing party like Reform which received 275,000 votes, 2.1 per cent of the national total, and no seats, in 1988. It may even be that regional districts, by strengthening regional party organizations, would help counteract rampant provincialism and improve regional integration in Western and Atlantic Canada.

A third possibility is to use the provinces as electoral districts. A fourth, the option recommended by Cassidy, is five-member districts. His calculations showed that they produce fairly good proportionality and, he suggests, they are more in keeping with Canada's tradition of viewing members of Parliament as local representatives. The Cassidy option, which he calls moderate proportional representation, would work well enough for the Liberals and Conservatives and the NDP in all but its weakest areas. However the effect of using small electoral districts, whether five-member ridings or small provinces, is to make it unlikely that parties getting less than 10 per cent of the vote would ever win a seat.

In a five-member riding, for example, the simplest PR formula assigns a seat to a party for each full 20 per cent of the vote it receives. The seats go to winning party candidates in the order they were presented on the party's list. Remaining seats are then assigned in order of the largest vote remainders. It is possible for a third or fourth party with as much as 12 per cent of the vote to get no seat.

There are several other formulas used for seat allocation in PR systems. Some confer an advantage on the largest party, some on medium-sized parties, and some on small parties. The formulas all give much the same outcome when the constituency magnitude is large and different outcomes when it is small. We think these are problems worth avoiding and that five-member constituencies are too small for genuine proportional representation.

THE GERMAN MODEL

The Federal Republic of Germany has an electoral system which ingeniously combines the appearance of British constituency voting with the results of proportional representation — a mixed system sometimes known as personalized proportional representation. This is the brand of PR nominated by New Zealanders as the reform alternative to British voting rules.

In Germany half the members of the Bundestag are elected in the British and Canadian fashion from single-member constituencies. To compensate for the resulting distortions, however, the other half are named from party lists in such way that each party's final share of seats corresponds closely to its national popular vote. For example if the Christian Democrats run strong in many constituencies and win on minority votes they will not be entitled to fill many extra seats from their list. Parties like the pivotal Free Democrats and a recent arrival, the Green Party, aren't strong enough to win constituency campaigns but are able to accumulate their minority vote from all over the country and acquire a substantial share of the compensatory list seats.

German voters mark their ballots twice — once for a local candidate and once for a national party. A rising fraction of the electorate, now about 15 per cent, splits the ballot by choosing a preferred major party candidate at the constituency level and a different party, such as the Free Democrats or Greens, in what is really the politically decisive vote, the list vote. Parties put favored constituency candidates on their list to increase their chances of reaching the Bundestag by one route or the other.

There are two refinements worthy of note. Germany, a federal state like Canada, requires that the party lists be drawn up by Land or province and that list seats be allocated on the same basis to encourage balanced regional representation and active regional organizations within each political party. Regional lists are also the practice in Austria, Belgium, Iceland, Italy, The Netherlands, Norway, Sweden, Denmark, Finland and Switzerland. The Germans, remembering the ghastly record of Adolf Hitler's National Socialist party and its small beginnings, for many years did not allow parties to win list seats unless they first won at least 5 per cent of the national vote or three constituency seats.[17] In Canada an explicit threshold barrier of that sort would likely be deemed a violation of the Charter of Rights.

Among the PR countries Germany is remarkable for its small number of political parties. In 1987 the Christian Democrats (34.5 per cent) and their longtime Bavarian ally, the Christian Social Union (9.8 per cent) were the largest electoral alliance. The Social Democrats won 37 per cent of the vote, the Free Democrats 9.1 per cent, the Green Party 8.3 per cent, and the National Democratic Party 0.6 per cent. In 1990 the Green Party fell just short of the 5 per cent threshold and lost all its seats.

PERSONALIZED PR FOR CANADA

The German-style system can be transferred to Canada, but it will require some changes in the way we do our political business. Assuming that we do not want to increase the number of Members of Parliament beyond 295, we can create a pool of seats to achieve proportional representation only by reducing the number of constituency MPs and increasing the population and territory of the remaining constituencies. Cassidy presents three simulations of the 1988 election in which 50 per cent, 33 per cent or 20 per cent of the House's 295 seats are allocated from a compensatory list to correct departures from proportional representation.

Cassidy suggests that any of the simulated options are acceptable but he prefers restricting the number of compensating seats to around 20 per cent of the total or 60 seats, the same number proposed by Pepin-Robarts and the Macdonald Commission.

His stated reason for choosing the 20 per cent figure is to keep the single-member constituencies as close as possible to present-day sizes. The unstated assumptions appear to be that the Liberal and Conservative leaderships can be persuaded to accept a mild

---

17   Hand, G., Georgel, J. and Sasse, C., *European Electoral Systems Hand-book*, 1979, pp. 58-86

Table 3.1

Comparison of Three Mixed Electoral Systems for Canada
1988 Federal Election

	PC	Lib	NDP	Reform	Other	Index of variance*
Actual seats	169	83	43	0	0	
Simulated seats						
50-50	130	97	60	6	2	
66-33	133	95	60	5	2	
80-20	143	89	59	3	1	
Actual Votes (%)	43	32	20	2	2	
Actual Seats (%)	57	28	15	0	0	14
Simulated seats (%)						
50-50	44	33	21	2	0.9	2
66-33	45	32	20	2	0.8	2
80-20	48	30	20	1	0.3	5

*The index of variance is a measure of departure from proportional representation. It is calculated by taking the difference, in percentage points, between a party's vote share and share of seats, adding the figures for all parties (without regard to sign) and dividing by two (because total gains equal total losses).

PR reform which removes some but not all of their unfair electoral advantage, that any of the reforms will benefit the NDP equally, and that all the other interests of women, social minorities and smaller political parties can safely be ignored.

We see it differently. Since 1978 and 1979, when federal NDP leader Ed Broadbent and Pepin-Robarts floated balloons much like Cassidy's, exactly nothing has happened. The Lortie royal commissioners, presumably acting on instructions from their party leaders, deliberately avoided any recommendation for proportional representation in the House of Commons. So no matter how much Cassidy, Broadbent or other federal New Democrats may wish it, the two dominant federal parties can't be coaxed or soft-soaped into changing the rules of the electoral game. Instead a citizen's movement will have to force one or another of the big parties to call a referendum on PR against its will. In that campaign the rallying call for the citizen's movement will not be "May we have a little bit of PR, please." It will be more like "Real Democrats Want Real PR." If mixed or German-style PR is the popular choice it will be the 50-50 version, not the 80-20 model.

The difference may not seem great to New Democrats, but they're only a fraction of the broad coalition that will take up the PR cause. Many of the activists will be people now associated with minority parties and non-establishment interest groups who are tired of being completely shut out of political decision-making — the women's movement, ethnic groups and visible minorities, disaffected Liberals and Tories, members of the National Party and the Green Party, the Communists, the Libertarians, Christian Heritage, and the Confederation of Regions. The coalition will include members of the Reform Party once they give up the pipedream of majority government. To these Canadians there is a world of difference between 60 compensatory seats and 150. The compensatory PR list is where all parties will find more room for talented women and minority candidates who now have difficulty obtaining nominations and winning elections in the constituencies. From that point of view, the bigger the list share of the House of Commons, the better.

For the majority of the population, the immediate appeal of proportional representation and the reason to vote for it in a referendum is that the resulting coalition governments, whether Liberal-NDP or Liberal-Conservative, are likely to be more closely in tune with the mood and thinking of a majority of the electorate.

For many of the democratic activists who will organize the Democracy League campaign, however, restricted forms of PR that create high barriers to small parties will hold little attraction. They will favor unrestricted PR because of its potential to expand the range of democratic debate in Canada and to give successful small parties the possibility of real influence. From time to time it is likely that a large party will find it necessary to talk seriously with small-party MPs to assemble a working majority and form a government. In our view that will be democracy working properly, because minorities should not be ignored if there is some reasonable way in which they can be accommodated.

YOU AND YOUR MEMBER OF PARLIAMENT

In mixed or personalized PR, the consequence of putting 150 House of Commons seats into the PR compensatory pool is to double the size of the electorate in each of the remaining territorial ridings. In straight PR the traditional ridings are eliminated because, as previously described, the electoral districts must contain large populations and dispose of large numbers of House of Commons seats to achieve a close approximation to proportional representation.

Consequently, during the debates on electoral reform, critics of PR will accuse reformers of attacking the vital democratic link between the people in a riding and their Member of Parliament. As we learned in Chapters One and Two, however, there is little reason to wax romantic about the relationship between voters and MPs. The attachment in fact is tenuous and in no way an adequate foundation for the entire political system. From the election of 1980 to the election of 1984 fully 53 per cent of the House of Commons incumbents disappeared, 31 per cent by defeat and 22 per cent by retirement. The changeover from 1984 to 1988 was almost as high — 42 per cent, of whom 22 per cent were defeated and 20 per cent retired.[18]

---

18   Ferejohn, J. and Gaines, B., The Personal Vote in Canada, RC Research Studies, Vol. 14, p. 281

In the United States the personal vote has become such a powerful factor that congressional incumbents are almost impossible to beat, but nothing like the same loyalties have formed between Canadians and their MPs. The Canadian Parliament is more like a glorified electoral college. Canadians watch national television news and vote for parties and prime ministers, and the MP is simply the vehicle through which the real political choice must be expressed.[19] A further indication of the weakness of the MP-constituent relationship, despite large increases in spending to provide MPs with constituency staff, is the continuing large number of swing seats. About 42 per cent of Canadian MPs won their seats in 1988 by a margin of 10 per cent or less, and 25 per cent by a margin of 5 per cent or less. These figures have been stable since 1925, indicating that many MPs find it impossible to build large personal followings and safe seats for themselves and their party.

Many backbench and opposition MPs shuttle frantically back and forth between House duty in Ottawa and casework duty in their ridings, but their immersion in casework and the study of airline schedules really reflects nothing more than their lack of serious responsibility in the capital. Canadians should not deny themselves an urgently needed electoral reform for fear that there will be no one to perform local social services. The pursuit of pension and unemployment insurance cheques and all the other prodding of the federal bureaucracy now offered by constituency MPs could probably in most cases be done better by a beefed-up federal Ombudsman's office with trained staff — people who stay on the job long enough to figure out how to get results and who aren't always exhausted from jet lag.

OTHER POSSIBLE VOTING REFORMS

We have indicated two versions of voting reform which should be offered to Canadians as choices on a referendum ballot — personalized PR with 150 list seats and straight PR by region.

---

19   Ibid. p. 277

We are not attracted to other options which have received serious attention from PR advocates — in particular Cassidy's proposal for PR within five-member electoral districts. Others may take a different view and five-member districts could end up as one of the choices on the ballot. There are other types of voting reform which we do not recommend because in our view they do not offer the advantages of party list PR. For the sake of completeness we will describe them briefly and indicate why they wouldn't help us get at the problems which need to be solved.

Preferential or Alternative Voting. Voters in single-member constituencies can be asked to indicate their preferences in rank order — 1,2,3 etc. Then, if no candidate wins an absolute majority, the candidate with the lowest vote is dropped and the ballots are distributed to the remaining candidates according to the second choices marked on them. The process continues until some candidate attains a majority.

This exercise gives the MP a greater aura of legitimacy but is very hard on third parties such as the NDP and Reform. The New Democrats, especially in Ontario, rely on split voting to get the seats they now win. Under preferential voting they would lose some of them because Liberal voters are more likely to vote Conservative, and Conservatives are more likely to vote Liberal, than NDP. All this adds up to an even greater departure from proportional representation.[20] Based on voter preference studies, an analysis of 1988 voting suggests that preferential voting would have strongly benefited the Liberal party to the disadvantage of Conservatives as well as New Democrats. Preferential voting offers no solution to the large discrepancy between the expressed first choices of Canadian voters and the allocation of seats in the House

---

20   Cassidy, op. cit., p. 29

of Commons, nor to the problem of regional imbalance in party representation.

Single Transferable Ballot. This elaborate voting system, championed a century ago by John Stuart Mill and now recommended for Canada by *The Globe and Mail*,[21] gives maximum effect to every ballot and a maximum range of choice to the voter without the slightest consideration for the interests or needs of political parties. It uses multi-seat constituencies and a ballot on which the voter ranks as many of the candidates as possible in order of preference. Once the total number of ballots is known, the electoral authority calculates the quota needed to win a seat. In a five-member riding, for example, the quota is one-sixth of the ballots plus one. The reasoning is that if four candidates reach the winning quota a fifth cannot. If no candidate reaches quota on the first count, the bottom candidate is dropped and the ballots are distributed to other candidates according to the second preferences marked. When a candidate reaches the quota he or she is declared elected and any surplus ballots in the winner's tally are distributed to the remaining candidates in suitable proportion. The process continues until four candidates are elected and no further redistribution can affect the ranking of the remaining candidates. The one with the highest total at that point is the fifth and final member elected.

The counting of an STV ballot can be slow. In Ireland voters sometimes wait several days for results after a general election, but they are well entertained by news reports of the progress of the count at each step.[22] STV allows a voter to express a series of preferences for candidates within a party as well as independents and candidates in other parties, knowing that the ballot will never

---

21 An editorial on June 12, 1993 addressed to Conservative convention delegates said: "We have to reconnect Canadians to their system of government. The biggest single improvement would be reform of the electoral system, perhaps along transferable ballot lines, to forestall the false majorities and regional ghettoes produced by the present first-past-the-post system."

22 Lakeman, E., *How Democracies Vote*, 1970, p. 105

help a candidate of whom the voter does not approve. It's like having party primary elections or nomination contests built right into the general election ballot. The voter need never think about negative or strategic voting, and proportional representation of all competing interests is achieved within the limits imposed by the number of seats at stake. Constituency magnitudes must be large enough to allow for a variety of representation, and yet not so large as to render the ballot ridiculous. In a five-member constituency, for example, a contest with five parties and independents can confront the voter with a ballot listing 30 or more names.

One voter option is simply to vote for five members of the same political party, but even in that case the order in which they are chosen is important. The STV system emphasizes the personal characteristics of the candidates and encourages competition among candidates of the same party as well as among the parties. In our view STV is a good voting system for elections in any small organization or even a city council but because of the limitations of constituency magnitude we don't think it's the best way to choose legislators for a continent-spanning state. On the other hand, it's better than the way we do it now. In a referendum choice among options for voting reform, an STV model should be on the ballot.

Those of us who want proportional representation and who believe the public will choose it when given the chance still have some obstacles to overcome. How to get a referendum when the established political parties don't want one is not self-evident. And even if they agree to a referendum, the structuring of the questions is critical. Voters asked to choose between British rules and reform, for example, will choose reform. But put British rules and four or five different voting reform options against each other on the same ballot and British rules might win a plurality. To be sure that a referendum's purpose is to advance the cause of reform fairly and not to derail it, we need to be in control of the referendum design. This leads us to consider the other important cause of the Democracy League — the citizen Initiative.

4

THE POLITICS OF INCLUSION: CITIZEN LAWMAKING

*The majority of the plain people will,
day in and day out, make fewer mistakes
in governing themselves than any smaller
body of men will make in trying to govern them.*

—Theodore Roosevelt

*The devices of direct democracy are not foreign
to the Canadian political tradition.
They are only foreign to a reactionary, elitist doctrine
of parliamentary politics enunciated in
Great Britain some 200 years ago by Edmund Burke.*

— Michael Bliss, historian, University of Toronto

*I'm not big on the idea of referendums generally.
I think the British parliamentary system
provides for our elected MPs to make up their mind.*

— Prime Minister Brian Mulroney, 1986

*If ever we have to ask questions
we will do it with great precision.
There will be no flim-flam in it.*

— Prime Minister Brian Mulroney, 1991

W E CANADIANS ARE PASSIVE and unhappy spectators in our own democracy as we vote once every four — or five — years, hope for the best, and get much less. A reform of Canada's unfair election voting rules will do a lot to improve representation and lessen our discontents but more is needed to give lasting legitimacy to our elite-dominated political system. There are limitations to all representative democracy which can be offset only by a strong shot of direct democracy — the kind in which citizens debate and decide, bypassing the usual brokering, filtering and hijacking of the issues by pressure groups, lobbyists, politicians and political parties.

Canada can't practise democracy in the manner of the city state of ancient Athens or the New England town hall assembly because the face-to-face meeting simply can't be the main device for governing 26 million people spread over half a continent. But the underlying democratic idea — that most citizens are able to assess debates on major questions of public choice and make reasonable decisions, and that their verdicts will be more palatable in most cases than the decisions of elites — is gaining ground again as the institutions of representative democracy discredit themselves.

A *Maclean's*-Decima poll published in 1991 showed that a huge majority of Canadians wants government to consult the public before making major decisions — 67 per cent in British Columbia, 76 per cent in the Prairies, 80 per cent in Ontario, 75 per cent in Quebec and 84 per cent in Atlantic Canada. Most of us know that government is already addicted to opinion polling and we mean something more specific, more muscular, more obligatory, when we ask for consultation.

Prime Minister Kim Campbell has tried to align herself with this public mood by talking during her rise to leadership about a new way of doing politics. "I am committed to bringing a new approach to government: the politics of inclusion that stresses listening to and involving people in their government," she said while introducing her proposals for democratic reform. "Our politics...has become the politics of elites — a politics of exclusivity, insiders, privilege and influence. The politics of inclusion...is a politics in which the balance of democratic power rests with the citizenry."

The referendum[1] in its various forms is the most obvious way to include all the citizens of a mass democracy — even those "apathetic SOBs" who don't agree with Campbell — in political decision-making.

The two most important tools of direct democracy, the Initiative — a citizen-initiated popular vote on a citizen-proposed question or statute — and the Referendum — a citizen-initiated popular vote on a new law adopted by Parliament — are the remedies of last resort for a public frustrated by an unresponsive government. They allow the people to circumvent a legislature blockaded by special interests, to enact needed reforms ignored by the government, and even to limit the basic powers of government itself.

There are, however, some other more limited and manipulative versions of direct democracy in the wind of which we will want to be wary. Financial Post editor Diane Francis recently told Campbell that the politics of inclusion cannot mean just more involvement with noisy special interest groups and people who join political parties and knock on doors. To be successful, Francis advised, Campbell's vision must take in all those who raise families, put in a fair day's work in the factory or meeting sales quotas and don't find it useful to join political parties — in other words, the vast majority of Canadians. "These are the people who are asked for their opinion every four or five years but are forced to pay the tab daily," said Francis. They can be included, she advised, "with routine referendums on major social and economic issues."[2] Francis thinks the referendum can be used by Ottawa to build consensus on the debt and deficit problem "because it allows politicians to pass the buck. Voters should be forced to make the choices: cut

---

1   The semantic distinctions among various forms of direct voting have been so thoroughly fudged that there's little point trying to reassert them. The essential distinctions are whether the procedure is commenced by law, by the legislature or by citizens, and whether the result is advisory to the government or becomes law.

2   *Financial Post*, June 15, 1993

or tax. They should be told the consequences." Without such referendums, she says, no politician will be able to make the tough decisions. "Instead they will have to be machiavellian and equivocal, speaking out of both sides of their mouths and talking deficit reduction without specifics." Such politicians cannot win public trust, she concludes, "but a politician who pledges to create a structure of guaranteed participation can win." Francis did not spell out the referendum questions she has in mind but it is unlikely that she intends referendum voting on Ottawa's major economic legislation. In any case Prime Minister Campbell seems to understand that Francis' plan for more government-sponsored referendums will quickly lead to demands for Referendum and Initiative — votes when the people want them and on subjects chosen by the people rather than votes at the convenience of the government.

Campbell, although silent on referendums, has already presented herself as a friend of the Initiative. She acknowledges, in principle, that a real politics of inclusion is possible only when some laws can come directly from citizens and be adopted by popular vote without having to go through the parliamentary mill. This direct procedure would give us a valuable tool for restraining or prodding the elites and Parliament as need be, and in our view should be the top priority of Canadian democrats. The electoral reforms proposed in Chapter Three, for example, are unlikely to become law unless the law is proposed and adopted directly by the people of Canada. This fact alone makes any discussion by a major party leader of the Initiative, the key to all other reforms, a matter of great interest.

As a British Columbian Campbell knows that voters in her own province gave massive support to the concept of the Initiative in a 1991 plebiscite. Speaking during her leadership campaign on the topic of empowering Canadians she said:

> I believe the time has come to seriously consider the issues surrounding citizens' intitiatives. On one hand permitting a sufficient number of interested individuals to force a referendum on issues of interest to them would put significant power back in the hands of

the Canadian people. On the other hand, there are legitimate concerns to be addressed about the predominance of majoritarian principles in a country where regional equity, the fair treatment of language and other minorities, the reconciliation of special interests into a national consensus, and the regulation of the political power of money, are integral to our national philosophy.

Now that this straight shooter from the West has taken the initiative, so to speak, we need to understand clearly whether she's for it or against it. The first clue is the vagueness of the pledge: "A parliamentary task force should be charged with engaging Canadians in a discussion of the issues surrounding citizens' initiatives and presenting the conclusions to Parliament." The second is Campbell's definition of the number of citizen signatures she would consider sufficient to trigger a referendum vote: "5 per cent of the registered voters in each province and territory." On the 1988 figure of 17.6 million eligible voters that will require an absolute minimum of 880,000 signatures, and provision for extra signatures to protect against disqualifications will push the real signature requirement to nearly 1,000,000. The further requirement that the signatures come proportionately from every jurisdiction in Canada will add substantially to the challenge, making an Initiative vastly expensive and well-nigh impossible to organize. As a threshold for this type of serious, substantive communication between the people and the national government, Campbell has proposed a guaranteed stopper.

The prime minister is certainly not alone in her mistrust of direct democracy. To most members of Canada's establishment referendums of any kind, even government-sponsored, are a measure of last resort and the fate of the Charlottetown Accord reminds us why. The proposals for constitutional change came forward endorsed by among others Brian Mulroney, Jean Chrétien, Audrey McLaughlin and their parties, all the provincial premiers, two territorial leaders, four aboriginal leaders, the Business Council on National Issues and the Canadian Labor Congress. The people considered them, and a majority of 54 per cent voted No. Referendums definitely allow citizens to reclaim some of their sovereign democratic power from representatives, and that is precisely their virtue.

Referendums sponsored by Parliament are always intended to help the prime minister and government out of a tight spot, but it's by no means clear they always work that way. Canada's 1992 experience proves that even an advisory referendum on constitutional change can have a significant impact on the operations of our democracy. We can no longer imagine the prime minister and premiers rolling the dice in another game of constitutional craps without submitting their final proposals to the people by referendum. The certainty that they will have to do that will make them reluctant to try the exercise again, and Canada will be better for their abstinence. In effect, and without a comma being changed, the constitutional practice of Canada has been substantially amended by one discretionary and non-binding referendum.

NATIONAL REFERENDUMS: ENDANGERED SPECIES

Parliament's desire to consult the people on a specific issue is so rarely aroused that there have been only three national referendums since Confederation: on prohibition in 1898, on conscription in 1942, and on the Charlottetown Accord package of constitutional changes in 1992. When Parliament wants or needs a referendum, it passes specific legislation and holds one. The people's desire to consult with Parliament arises much more frequently, largely due to the unrepresentative character of our majority governments. They generally begin life lacking the support of a majority of the population and go on to govern by their own lights for periods up to five years. Some prime ministers like Brian Mulroney pretend to an all-encompassing mandate to govern, a sort of blank cheque conferred by their control of Parliament. More careful leaders may try to restrict controversial actions to those policies actually set out in their election programs, but even that limited version of the mandate doctrine is, in the end, not really acceptable. Canadian elections are about leaders, their teams and their general political orientation and only incidentally about specific policies. It is entirely possible, especially given the very loose link between popular vote and seat allocation, for a party to attain a majority in Parliament in spite of and not because of some of its stated policies.

Canada's free trade debate highlighted the emptiness of the mandate doctrine of government in every possible way.[3] Brian Mulroney's Conservatives, armed with 50 per cent of the popular vote, 75 per cent of the MPs, and no specific mandate on the issue from the voters, entered free trade talks and reached a tentative agreement with the United States. NDP leader Ed Broadbent was the first to urge, in 1987, that the Prime Minister "let the people decide" the fate of the free trade agreement. This was a figure of speech indicating that the NDP was riding high in the polls at the time and Broadbent wouldn't mind if Mulroney called a general election. As Conservative MP Patrick Boyer said at the time, a general election can't be confined to one issue "so if anyone genuinely wants to take the free trade issue to the Canadian people the only way to do it is a national plebiscite."[4]

In mid-1988 Liberal leader John Turner also challenged Mulroney to let the people decide the free trade issue and his notion of how that should be done was identical to Broadbent's. Turner encouraged Liberal senators to block the free trade legislation and forced a general election. The ensuing campaign centred on the trade deal and its implications for the economy, the environment, social programs and Canadian sovereignty but the outcome was also influenced by voter attitudes on tax reform, child care, nuclear submarines, abortion, the deficit, western alienation, fishing quotas, parole administration, pension adjustments and a range of serious environmental concerns.

Broadbent and Turner both said the trade deal was bad for Canada but did not unite to oppose the Conservatives and in that way gave Mulroney an important edge: a major issue, the country equally divided, and his the only party on one side of the controversy. The Conservatives won a deep-discount 43 per cent

---

3   Boyer, P. *The People's Mandate,* 1992, pp. 87-136
4   Ibid. p. 128

majority government. Free trade became law. The other parties, with 57 per cent of the vote, stayed on the opposition benches. The size of the opposition vote, as Boyer points out, does not represent the public verdict on free trade and we'll never know what it would have been. Political scientists working on the Canadian National Election Study say that 80 per cent of those polled had a definite opinion on free trade and 90 per cent voted in accordance with that opinion, but no clear majority emerged because a significant minority never did make up its mind.

Ironically, the election strategy adopted by the Liberals and NDP on the free trade issue would have accomplished a change of government had they been operating under proportional representation voting rules. In the first-past-the-post world in which they were actually living, however, it made little sense to polarize the election on a single issue without providing for voting alliances between Liberals and New Democrats in the ridings.[5] The campaign raised emotions and expectations among the Canadian people which the business-as-usual opposition tactics could not accommodate, and the discrepancy effectively ended the careers of both opposition leaders.

Broadbent or Turner, had they wanted to isolate the free trade issue from the rest of the general election agenda, might have asked for a referendum but Prime Minister Mulroney, with partisan advantage in hand, would have scoffed at the very idea. No matter how much a referendum might serve the national interest, an opposition party leader can't initiate one in Canada nor can any ordinary citizen or organized group. National referendums remain another of the exclusive prerogatives of the leader of the governing party, the prime minister of Canada.

---

5   It made little sense if the concern was the impact of free trade on Canada. It made great sense if the real issue was simply which of the two parties would become the official opposition. Turner forced the free trade issue and increased his party's popularity at the expense of the NDP. One election later, the Liberals are poised to become the government and the NDP is facing oblivion.

REFERENDUMS IN PRACTICE

Many countries use referendums occasionally to deal with constitutional issues as did the United Kingdom in 1975 to decide whether to join the European Economic Community. But among nation-states only Switzerland uses the mandatory or binding referendum as standard device in the regular operation of its federal government. All laws and decrees in Switzerland may be challenged if within 90 days of publication 50,000 citizens sign a petition demanding a referendum. Unless the federal assembly declares a matter urgent, legislation does not come into force until the referendum vote is completed. Government legislation is usually crafted to survive the popular vote and citizen initiatives, almost always inspired by minority interests, are usually defeated. Government often reacts with follow-up legislation which incorporates some of the petitioners' objectives.[6]

The public in other countries has been called upon to decide important questions from time to time. Spanish citizens voted to remain in the North Atlantic Treaty Organization. The Irish and Italians voted on divorce, and the mere threat of a citizen initiative forced the Italian government to grapple with legalizing abortion. The most extensive use of referendums outside Switzerland, however, is found at the state level in the United States. Twenty-two states provide for some form of citizen-initiated referendum. Most of them lie west of the Mississippi where the direct democracy tradition is the legacy of the Populist Party and the sweeping activities of the Progressive movement from the turn of the century into World War I. The most active practitioners of the Initiative have been the citizens of Oregon, California, North Dakota, Colorado and Arizona. The subjects range from government and political process, public morality, revenue, taxation and borrowing to regulation of business and labor, health, welfare, housing, civil liberties and rights, education, environment and land use plan-

---

6   Butler, D. and Ranney, A. *Referendums : A Comparative Study of Practice and Theory,* p. 41

ning. In 1912, for example, Arizona voted 68 per cent in favor of giving women the vote. In 1975 Washington voted 68 per cent for a mandatory death penalty in cases of aggravated first degree murder. In 1986 California voters defeated a proposal by followers of Lyndon LaRouche to quarantine carriers of the AIDs virus.

A survey of 18 states showed voters approving 34 per cent of proposals initiated by popular petition and 60 per cent of proposals, mainly constitutional, proposed by the state legislatures. This suggests that voters in most states are more likely to think well of a proposed new law or constitutional amendment if it has been considered and approved by elected representatives and are prudently skeptical of the proposal of special interest and public interest pressure groups. In other words, direct legislation by referendum is not perceived as an alternative to representative democracy but as a useful supplement to the basic machinery.[7] An important exception to this generalization is California, where the state governor and legislature are often at loggerheads and Initiatives have become, in the words of one political consultant, "the main way to get big things done."[8] During the 1980s half the 44 ballot-proposed initiatives put to California voters were approved, leading some observers to suggest that the Initiative had become a fourth branch of government. The voters made changes in nearly every aspect of California life: reduced property taxes; eliminated gift and inheritance taxes; indexed income taxes; adopted a state lottery; enacted campaign finance reform; guaranteed school funds; raised tobacco taxes; regulated toxic materials; rolled back auto insurance rates; reformed the criminal justice system; protected wildlife; and adopted term limits for state elected officials.[9]

---

7   Ibid. p. 70. They are Maine, Massachusetts, Florida, Michigan, Ohio, Missouri, Nebraska, North Dakota, South Dakota, Arkansas, Oklahoma, Arizona, Colorado, Nevada, California and Oregon.
8   David Townsend, quoted in *California Business*, Feb. 1990
9   California Commission on Campaign Financing, *Democracy by Initiative*, 1992, p. 10

In California and elsewhere in the U.S. the Initiative has not provided any consistent advantage to either the liberal or conservative political agendas. American right-wingers like Pat Buchanan and Kevin Phillips have viewed direct democracy as a way to free conservative voters from the grips of a liberal conspiracy among legislators, executives, bureaucrats and controllers of the mass media. The tax revolt heralded by California's Proposition 13 in 1978 seemed to vindicate that hope as voters went beyond previous unsuccessful proposals by former California governor Ronald Reagan, capped the property tax rate at 1 per cent, and severely limited the state's power to finance public services from that source. Tax revolt initiatives also passed in Idaho in 1978 and Massachussetts in 1980, but similar initiatives were voted down in 16 other states between 1978 and 1984. The main effect of the tax revolt where it succeeded seems to have been an increase in state financial transfers to local government and a proliferation of user fees for public services.[10] Voters, however, have rejected several subsequent direct attempts by the legislature and public sector unions to weaken the tax limitation.

When Senator James Abourezk, a Democrat from South Dakota, proposed national Initiative and Referendum legislation in 1977, his support came not from conservatives but from environmentalists and liberals including Ralph Nader. Arguing the eventually unsuccessful case for direct legislation a leader of Initiative America made this pitch:

> Florida and California have strict political honesty laws on the books; Missouri law now protects customers from unfair utility charges; North Dakota has outlawed huge corporate farming in their state; Michigan and Maine are saving energy and stopping litter with returnable bottles and cans; and a California initiative enabled

---

10   Zimmerman, J., *Participatory Democracy: Populism Revived*, 1986, p. 87

the legislature to pass a nuclear waste disposal law against what had previously been strong lobbying efforts by power companies.[11]

In the United States, while direct democracy conservatives put their energies into the tax revolt, the left in 1982 waged what quickly became a nation-wide campaign for a U.S.-Soviet nuclear weapons freeze and later evolved into a campaign for nuclear-free zones at the state and municipal level. The freeze campaign, as close as the U.S. has ever come to a national referendum, attracted 11.6 million supporters versus 7.9 million opposed and won in nine of ten U.S. states and 34 of 37 U.S. cities and counties where citizens initiated referendums. It didn't stop the House of Representatives from voting to proceed with the MX missile, but may have been a contributing factor in President Ronald Reagan's subsequent decision to negotiate arms control with the tottering Soviet regime.

The early nuclear-free zone initiatives — Cambridge in 1983, Ann Arbour and Santa Monica in 1984 — lost about 60-40 but Nuclear Free America described them as "tremendous successes," engaging the communities in vigorous debate and "forcing them to assess their own role in the nuclear arms race and to take a stand, one way or the other."[12] By the end of 1988 a total of 160 U.S. towns, cities and counties with a combined population of 16 million were officially declared nuclear-free zones, and in a few like Marin County, California the accompanying ordinances were so strict that city officials couldn't buy cars from General Motors or light bulbs from General Electric because both had nuclear weapons contracts.

The overall U.S. referendum voting pattern since World War II has favored liberal positions on right-to-work and tax laws, conservative positions on the death penalty, abortion and race dis-

---

11   John Forster, director of Initiative America, cited in Butler and Ranney, op. cit., p. 83
12   Cited in Schmidt, David, *Citizen Lawmakers: The Ballot Initiative Revolution,* 1989, p. 156

crimination, and thoroughly mixed results on nuclear power development. "The referendum is neither an unfailing friend nor an implacable enemy of either left or right," concluded Austin Ranney of the American Enterprise Institute. "The policies that referendums produce depend on the state of public opinion at the time, and in a democratic polity voters lean right on some occasions and left on others."[13]

George Gallup Sr., after more than 50 years of public opinion polling, said in 1984: "The judgment of the American people is extraordinarily sound. The public is always ahead of its leaders." Gallup went on to endorse citizen-initiated lawmaking at the national level: "I think the country would have been a hell of a lot better governed over the past 50 years if we had national Initiative....On most major issues we've dealt with in the past 50 years the public was more likely to be right — based on the judgment of history — than the legislatures or Congress."[14]

A more cautious assessment is provided by Colorado professor Thomas Cronin in a book, *Direct Democracy,* prepared under sponsorship of the non-partisan Twentieth Century Fund. "The American experience with direct democracy has fulfilled neither the dreams and expectations of its proponents nor the fears of its opponents," he concludes. The virtues of extending Initiative and Referendum to the national level lie in the potential for getting citizens more interested and involved in the decision-making of the nation and are akin to "another extension of suffrage, a vote of confidence in the people." But, Cronin notes, the Initiative bypasses the elaborate division of powers in the U.S. political system which was based on elite mistrust of popular passions and "created some distance between the people and their leaders in order to provide some scope for leadership or statesmanship."[15] His most serious reservations arise from the potential for distortion and unfairness in national referendum campaigns due to

---

13   Butler and Ranney, op. cit.,. p. 85
14   Schmidt, op. cit., p. 40
15   Cronin, T. *Direct Democracy,* 1989, p. 188

probable massive imbalances in spending on the Yes and No sides, a problem reinforced by U.S. court decisions which, in the name of freedom of speech, prevent limitations on referendum campaign expenditures and contributions.

Canadians are well acquainted with both elite mistrust of the people and the problems created by money power in democratic politics. These are matters which must be faced and resolved as we design a citizen Initiative suitable for the parliamentary system of Canada and its provinces.

A SMIDGEN OF DIRECT DEMOCRACY

Prior to 1992 only two Canadian Prime Ministers, Wilfrid Laurier and Mackenzie King, had consulted the people by referendum. Laurier, who came to office in 1896 with commitments to the temperance movement, held a plebiscite in 1898 on this question: "Are you in favor of the passing of an Act prohibiting the importation, manufacture or sale of spirits, wine, ale, beer, cider and all other alcoholic liquors for use as beverages?"

Twenty years earlier Canada had adopted a law permitting prohibition on the basis of local votes, but opponents of the demon rum were hoping to wrap the whole thing up in one sweeping national measure. It was not to be. Even on principle only 51 per cent of Canadian voters favored prohibition, and within that total lurked *la difference*. Five of six Quebec voters were against the proposal while two of every three in the rest of the country favored it. Not surprisingly Laurier chose to do nothing and left the issue to the provinces where it inspired frequent referendums for the next three decades. The prohibitionists were disappointed in Laurier, but they had their day in court and learned exactly why it was impossible to devise a single policy to suit the whole country.[16] In 1917 Laurier, as leader of the opposition, again proposed a referendum to resolve a Canadian dilemma

---

16   Boyer, P. *Direct Democracy in Canada*, 1992, pp. 16-26

— a country badly divided over the need to conscript manpower for World War I. Sentiment against conscription ran strongly in Quebec and for it just as strongly in other parts of the country. Laurier urged a popular vote, arguing that many people across Canada, particularly in the laboring classes, opposed conscription and would never be reconciled to it without a democratic decision. Laurier was ignored, conscription proceeded, Robert Borden's Union government won re-election in 1917 with almost no seats in Quebec, and the Conservative party was toast in that province for decades afterwards.

In 1942 Mackenzie King faced a similar need to conscript manpower for war and a similarly divided country. He had tied his own hands by leading the Liberal party to victory in 1940, six months after the outbreak of World War II, with promises of a limited liability war and no conscription for overseas service. King's solution was to conduct a referendum in which the populace was asked: "Are you in favor of releasing the government from any obligation arising out of any past commitments restricting the methods of raising men for military service?" The outrage in Quebec was intense, because it was assumed the election pledge had been given to Quebec while all of Canada would be allowed to withdraw it.

In an immediate sense King's referendum didn't work. The Yes vote carried eight provinces with 69 to 82 per cent of the vote, but in Quebec 79 per cent of electors refused to release the Liberals from their obligation. Ultimately the direct vote was a master stroke because it showed Canadians again how deep their differences ran. In Ontario four voters in five supported conscription, while in Quebec four of every five opposed it. The split was even more severe when analyzed along strictly linguistic lines. In the wake of the referendum King's government was able to delay conscription two more years until 1944, maintain a successful war effort, avoid the lasting rancor of the World War I conscription crisis, and win re-election in 1945, albeit with a 10 point slippage in popular vote to 41 per cent.[17]

Pierre Trudeau, the pied piper of participatory democracy, was no advocate of referendums on ordinary legislation but he did, in 1978, propose a Canada Referendum Act when Ottawa needed to equip itself for a period of constitutional turbulence and strife with a Quebec government disposed to independence. The government of Canada needed within its "arsenal of available devices" a means to respond to a provincial vote on separation, Trudeau said, but the proposed law was not otherwise intended "to change in any sense our parliamentary system." Sole responsibility for legislation and policies was to remain with Parliament, which is to say the prime minister, and governments should not be permitted "to come forward with referendums to solve problems that the House of Commons or the government find too hot to handle."[18]

Trudeau's referendum proposal expired with his government in 1979 and no statute was available when he later contemplated a referendum to overcome federal-provincial disagreements during the negotiation of the Charter of Rights and other constitutional changes in 1982. As Patrick Boyer argues persuasively in *Direct Democracy in Canada,* Canada could only benefit from a permanent law providing for the conduct of referendums — referendums provoked by stalemate between the Senate and the Commons, referendums provoked by deadlock between Ottawa and the provinces, referendums necessitated by separatist voting in Quebec, or referendums on conscription, free trade and other major policies which change the direction of the country.

DIRECT DEMOCRACY IN THE PROVINCES

Referendums have been used more frequently in the provinces than at the national level but have never taken hold as a regular

17   Ibid. pp. 36-42
18   Ibid. p. 42

feature of government practice. Generally they have been non-binding votes, often dealing with the prohibition or regulation of alcohol or the administration of daylight saving time. Between 1912 and 1919 Saskatchewan, Alberta and British Columbia adopted Direct Legislation Acts and Manitoba an Initiative and Referendum Act but the provincial governments which bowed to the Progressive reform program didn't do it with any great enthusiasm. They simply sidestepped the fate of Manitoba Conservative Premier Rodmond Roblin who openly resisted the Progressive reforms as "a denial of responsible government and a form of degenerate republicanism" until his government was defeated in 1915.

The entire direct democracy experiment came to little. Saskatchewan dropped the project in 1913 after voters failed to turn out in sufficient numbers to ratify a weak bill. The Manitoba law, which included provisions for binding citizen initiatives, was challenged and in 1919 found unconstitutional by the Judicial Committee of the Privy Council in London on the pretext that it usurped the authority of the lieutenant governor. No legislative measure was ever submitted to voters in Manitoba under the act nor did they initiate even a single statute. The Manitoba government made no attempt to correct the alleged defect and British Columbia, obediently taking the Privy Council's cue, left its legislation unproclaimed.[19]

In subsequent decades there have been a few significant provincial plebiscites. The people of British Columbia voted in favor of public health insurance in 1937 after B.C. doctors waged a strong campaign against a plan proposed in 1936. But despite being re-elected and a 58 per cent public approval on the referendum question the Liberal provincial government of Dufferin Pattullo backed away from its confrontation with the medical profession — a decision which sent the Liberal party into long-term decline and opened the door to the CCF in British Columbia.

---

19   Ibid. p. 91

In Newfoundland there were two referendums in 1948 which concluded with the decision to join Confederation. In that same year Albertans voted on a proposed provincial takeover of the electrical power generating and distribution system — and stopped short by a margin of 151 votes out of 280,000 cast. Quebec in 1919 voted against prohibition while it was in vogue around the continent and gave itself a profitable notoriety as tourists flocked in and the province reaped millions from the sale of booze.

The most dramatic of the provincial referendums was Quebec's in 1980 when the perpetual quest for a free and independent Quebec within a strong and united Canada was actually put to provincial voters. They decided, 60 per cent to 40, not to authorize the Parti Quebecois to try to negotiate sovereignty-association with the rest of Canada.

In 1988 "Friends of the Island" campaigned strenuously against a federal proposal to build a bridge or tunnel linking Prince Edward Island to the mainland, while "Islanders for a Better Tomorrow" pushed the case for cheaper transportation and expanded tourism. After a thorough debate about the island way of life the modernizers carried the question as 59 per cent of voters authorized, in principle, the creation of a fixed link. Debate over the costs, benefits and environmental impact continues and construction of a proposed bridge hasn't yet begun.

CONSULTATION: AN ACT OF DESPERATION

After decades in which direct democracy at the federal and provincial level has been restricted to a few plebiscites, there have been some recent signs of a shift in practice. Governments on the verge of defeat, including the Mulroney Conservatives, the Saskatchewan Conservatives and the Social Credit in British Columbia, have started to consult the electorate directly.

The 1992 federal referendum on rewriting the constitution was the single most spectacular and high-impact venture, but two quieter provincial experiments have reinforced the likelihood that referendums will no longer be rare and isolated events.

Saskatchewan's Conservative government, having pushed its term to the limit in 1991, suddenly put three non-binding questions on the election-day agenda: "Should the government of Saskatchewan be required to introduce balanced budget legislation?" "Should the people of Saskatchewan approve, by referendum or plebiscite, any proposed changes to the Canadian constitution?" And, since abortions are legally performed in some Saskatchewan hospitals, "Should the Government of Saskatchewan pay for abortion procedures?" Neither Grant Devine's Conservatives nor Roy Romanow's NDP put much cash or energy into the referendum campaigns and they seemed to have little effect on the general election in which the NDP prevailed. Voters supported the balanced-budget proposition and concept of ratifying constitutional changes with 80 per cent majorities. About 62 per cent of voters opposed government financing of abortions. There has been no subsequent action by the new NDP government on a balanced-budget law or payments to hospitals for abortions.[20]

The electors of British Columbia, while voting in a general election in 1991, answered two questions. One proposed a non-binding citizen initiative: "Should voters be given the right, by legislation, to propose questions that the government of British Columbia must submit to voters by referendum?" The second responded to public concerns about the apparent corruption of several legislators: "Should voters be given the right by legislation to vote between elections for the removal of their member of the legislative assembly?" These bows to direct democracy by Premier Rita Johnson did not rescue the Social Credit government from a plunge to third-party status, but B.C. voters were pleased to accept the new influence offered. More than 83 per cent favored the citizen Initiative and 81 per cent the right of recall. A legislative committee is now holding public hearings and, going beyond the strict wording of the referendum, is reviewing the full range of

---

20   Ibid. p. 175

potential citizen initiative powers including the direct lawmaking option. Its report is expected before the end of 1993.

WHICH BRAND OF DIRECT DEMOCRACY?

The choices under consideration by B.C.'s select standing committee on election reform are, as Kim Campbell understood, of considerable interest to all of Canada. We may expect the experience of the nearby U.S. states and especially the superstate of California, which is similar in population and economic power to Canada, to loom large in the B.C. deliberations.

Of the two reforms the recall seems by far the least useful for Canadian purposes. Recall makes sense in the U.S. states where terms of office are fixed and the party system is too weak to exert much restraint on wayward elected officials, but those are not the conditions in Canada. The Reform Party of Canada has included the recall as part of its platform, but it is not an item which need occupy much of the attention or energies of Canadian democrats. Elected representatives who are caught at criminal activity can be dealt with by the law. Those found in serious conflicts of interest, even first ministers like former B.C. Premier Bill Vander Zalm, are generally brought to account by the normal political and electoral process without any need for special elections to hasten the reckoning. If, however, the motive of recall advocates is to punish representatives for failing to vote correctly then it is simply misguided. In the first-past-the-post system a member of the legislature often is elected by fewer than 50 per cent of the voters and then, unlike the U.S. system, is generally required to vote on party instructions. Allowing the supporters of defeated candidates in a riding to recall and defeat the general election winner would introduce another element of absurdity to a system already overburdened with it. This revelation came to William "Bible Bill" Aberhart, the first Social Credit premier of Alberta, in a blinding flash in 1937 just one year after he put a recall law on the books which neglected to specify the grounds upon which a member could be recalled. The first petition was filed from the riding of Okotoks-High River which was then represented by the premier himself. The Social Credit majority in the legislature immediately repealed the law retroactively and that was the beginning and end of the recall experiment in Alberta and in Canada.[21]

Recall elections are even more foreign to a proportional representation parliamentary system because the individual legislators no longer pretend to represent the entire community. Under a PR regime legislators are primarily responsible to their political party, its membership and its voters. Questions of deviation from party policy or party ethics are settled internally and a recall by the general electorate would be both contrary to the logic of the system and quite impractical.

THE INITIATIVE: CITIZEN LAWMAKING

The case for the Initiative was originally put forward in North America by Progressives like Robert M. La Follette campaigning against "the inexhaustible resources and deeply entrenched forces of special privilege." In Canada's west that meant the Canadian Pacific Railway's influence in Parliament just as in California the target was the Southern Pacific Railroad, the octopus whose tentacles reached into the state legislature, the press and the courts.

> For years the American people have been engaged in a terrific struggle with the allied forces of organized wealth and political corruption.... The people must have in reserve new weapons for every emergency if they are to regain and preserve control of their governments....Through the initiative, referendum and recall the people in any emergency can absolutely control. The initiative and referendum make it possible for them to demand a direct vote and repeal bad laws which have been enacted, or to enact by direct vote good measures which their representatives refuse to consider.[22]

---

21 Boyer, P., *The People's Mandate*, p. 33
22 From the *Political Philosophy of Robert M. Lafollette* cited in Zimmerman, op. cit. p. 69

California adopted a battery of direct legislation devices in 1911, most of which remain in use to the present day. The basic scheme allows citizens by petition to demand referendums on laws passed by the legislature, to propose constitutional amendments, and to propose ordinary statutes. To forestall tinkering by a hostile legislature the law provides that initiative statutes, once adopted, can be amended only with the approval of the electorate.

A successful petition requires signatures equalling 5 per cent of the total vote cast for candidates seeking the office of governor in the previous election, which in practice means about 400,000 signatures. The citizen sponsors of a measure submit the proposed legal draft to the attorney general who prepares a title and a summary in 100 words or less which must appear in readable type on each signature page of the petition. In some states the attorney general is required to advise would-be petitioners of technical or constitutional objections to the proposed statutory text within two weeks. The petition sponsors then have 150 days to circulate and file the signed documents. Once the signatures are verified (using statistical sampling techniques) the petition is qualified. In California the balloting takes place at the next state-wide election but no sooner than 131 days after the qualification. All in all the procedural calendar runs nearly a year from the date of the first notice.

In the first six decades of direct democracy in California citizens attempted 369 initiatives of which less than half, 155, qualified for the ballot. Of those 42, a little more than one quarter, became law.[23] Since then, both the frequency of Initiatives and the success rate have increased dramatically and so has the cost of Initiative campaigning, prompting the California Commission on Campaign Financing to put forward a comprehensive scheme to regulate it.

---

23   Butler and Ranney, op. cit., p. 91

Californians are deeply attached to the direct balloting tradition and will not give it up, the Commission said last year, but they want tougher disclosure rules and spending limits.

A CITIZEN INITIATIVE FOR CANADA[24]

Even in the U.S. states where direct democracy is part of the culture, 99 per cent of all laws are adopted by the legislatures on their sole responsibility without prompting by citizen initiative or challenge by a citizen referendum.[25] In the same vein a former prime minister of Canada, Arthur Meighen, observed that 98 per cent of Parliament's work has nothing to do with anything said to voters during the previous election campaign.

The tools of direct democracy do not replace legislatures but supplement and fix up their work where it is consistently lacking. Our guiding thought in what follows is not to make citizen initiatives a dime a dozen, but to make them reasonably possible. We see no compelling reason, for example, why issues of conscience such as the death penalty or abortion rules should be decided by free votes among 295 Members of Parliament. There are so many ways in which Parliament is not a mirror of Canadian society that it would be far more democratic to submit such non-partisan questions to a free vote of 17.6 million Canadian electors. All of us should be equally engaged in deciding what kind of society we are or are striving to be, and if Parliament doesn't extend us that right we should have a law which makes it possible for us to claim it.

A Canada Initiatives and Referendum Act would have these essential elements:

---

24   This section combines suggestions from various sources including David Schmidt's *Citizen Lawmakers*, Thomas Cronin's *Direct Democracy*, Benjamin Barber's *Strong Democracy*, reform proposals from the California Commission on Campaign Financing, and the private bill MP Patrick Boyer has submitted to the House of Commons every year since 1988.

25   Cronin, T., op. cit. p. 228

Statutory powers. A provision giving voters the power to propose and enact resolutions and laws which have the same force and effect as acts of Parliament.

Constitutional amendments. A provision giving voters the power to propose and enact amendments to the Constitution of Canada.

Restriction. No subject matter may be put to the voters by Initiative more than once during the life of a Parliament.

Veto power. A provision giving voters the power to block by petition and reject by popular vote new laws passed by Parliament.

Definitions and Qualifying Conditions. The Initiative would be proposed by presenting to the attorney general a petition setting forth the text of the proposed statute, resolution or amendment to the constitution and signed by electors equal in number to 3 per cent of the votes cast in the previous federal election in the case of ordinary legislation and 5 per cent in the case of an amendment to the constitution. Based on the 13.3 million votes cast in 1988, the qualifying threshold would be 400,000 signatures for regular statutes and 650,000 for constitutional amendments. No time limit less than 365 days shall be imposed for the circulation of an Initiative petition.

The Referendum is the power of electors to approve or reject statutes or parts of statutes except emergency statutes approved by three quarters of the House of Commons and of the Senate. It may be proposed by presenting to the chief electoral officer, within 90 days after the adjournment of the legislative session during which it was passed, a petition with signatures equal in number to 3 per cent of the votes cast in the last federal election asking that the statute or part of it be submitted to the electors. The chief electoral officer shall have 40 days to verify the signatures and shall submit the measure at the next suitably scheduled referendum voting date.

Effect of Referendums. If a Referendum petition is filed against part of a statute, the remainder of the statute shall not be delayed from going into effect. If two or more Initiative or Referendum measures approved at the same time conflict, those of the measure receiving the highest affirmative vote shall prevail.

Election dates. In the U.S. Initiatives and Referendums are voted at the same time as primary and general elections which occur on a fixed timetable. Combining the elections saves money and increases voter turnout. In Canada the Lortie commission and others have recommended that referendums be kept separate from general elections so they may be dealt with on their merits without confounding partisan influences.

We accept this view. Initiative and Referendum voting should be conducted annually in mid-fall on a predictable date to create a firm and reliable timetable for citizen petitioners. The cost of a stand-alone federal referendum can be kept to about $85 million, and shaved to $50 million if Ottawa develops, in cooperation with the provinces and municipalities, a permanent list of voters.[26] The costs can be further reduced by setting the voting date to coincide with regular municipal elections where possible to make use of that electoral machinery.

Deadlines. The petition filing deadline for an Initiative shall be at least 130 days prior to the election day to allow the chief electoral officer 40 days to verify signatures and interested parties a further three months after qualification to organize committees and wage campaigns for and against the Initiative.

Override. Initiative or Referendum voting shall be suspended if a federal election is called during a referendum campaign period. It is possible a new Parliament might address and resolve the issue raised on the direct ballot, but it is equally possible that it would not. To protect citizen lawmaking, an Initiative or Referendum suspended by an election shall be rescheduled for the next year's vote unless instructions to the contrary are received from a majority of the petition sponsors.

Amendment. An Initiative approved by electors may be amended by Parliament acting alone only if the citizen statute so provides. Otherwise amendments by Parliament shall be sub-

---

26   Boyer, P. *The People's Mandate*, p. 207

mitted to the electors for approval by a voting majority before going into effect.

Perfecting the Petition. Prior to the circulation of an Initiative or Referendum petition for signatures, the required 200 sponsors shall submit the precise wording of the proposed question or statutue to the attorney general who shall, within 10 working days, convene a drafting conference at which he or his agents shall provide written comments setting out possible difficulties with the language or constitutionality of the proposed statute. The sponsors may accept or reject the advice in whole or in part.

Titling. The attorney general shall present to the drafting conference a title and concise summary, not to exceed 100 words and not to be an argument or create prejudice for or against the measure, and shall print it on each petition form.

Pre-vote Hearings. Parliament shall hold a hearing on each initiative within 10 days after it qualifies for a ballot. Proponents will be allowed to amend the initiative to correct errors or make improvements so long as they are consistent with the original purpose and intent.

Negotiation Period. Parliament may within 45 days enact, with the approval of the Initiative proponents, a substitute measure and the proponents will then withdraw the Initiative. If Parliament's measures go beyond the purpose and intent of the Initiative, it can with the approval of the proponents place the substitute measure on the ballot.

Publication. The chief electoral officer shall publish a brief summary of all Intitiative and Referendum measures submitted to the people with fair arguments for and against the measures and a fair estimate of their possible cost and consequences and, at least 10 days before the voting, distribute a copy to the residence of each elector, and make such additional distributions as seem necessary to ensure that each voter will have an opportunity to study the measures prior to the vote. The CEO shall also produce and make generally available, at least 10 days before the voting, a broadcast-quality videotape for the same purpose.

Disputes. A Public Consultation Council composed of three judges of the Federal Court of Canada shall provide timely opinions on legal or technical questions arising from the use of this legislation and, upon request by either consultation committee, render final, binding decisions.

Multi-choice ballot. The ballot, instead of offering only the choices of Yes and No, shall offer strong and weak versions of each to allow both proponents and opponents to understand the nature of public attitudes and guide future actions accordingly. The choices shall be: Yes, strongly support; Yes, with reservations; No, strongly oppose; No, reformulate; and No, postpone.[27]

Two Votes. An Initiative approved on the first ballot shall be rescheduled for a confirming final vote the following year. In the meantime Parliament may adopt legislation on the matter in question. A majority of the petition sponsors, if satisfied by Parliament's response, may withdraw the Initiative from the ballot. If they do not both the Initiative and Parliament's bill shall appear on the ballot and the one receiving the largest majority affirmative vote shall be the law.

Execution. If in the opinion of the Supreme Court of Canada it is necessary, Parliament shall give an Initiative approved by the electors three readings within a week of its final approval, submit it to the Governor General for royal assent, and proclaim it within five days of receiving the assent. Otherwise, an act shall be submitted to the Governor General for royal assent within five days of final approval by a majority of electors and shall be deemed proclaimed when that assent is given. Parliament may enact legislation to facilitate its operation. Manitoba's direct democracy legislation was struck down in 1919 because it allegedly interfered with the prerogatives of the lieutenant governor and until a case is heard by the Supreme Court of Canada this remains the law. Alberta repealed its little-used statute on the same reasoning 40 years later. The British Columbia legislative committee studying the Initiative had not formed an opinion about the constitutionality of direct legislation as we were writing.

---

27   Barber, Benjamin, *Strong Democracy*, 1984, p. 286

Patrick Boyer said the Manitoba case established that "a provincial legislature cannot make general provision for plebiscites or referendums that are legislatively self-executing." It must make the referendum advisory, he said, "so the subsequent execution of the change would still be at the discretion of the provincial legislature." Of course, the whole point of direct democracy is to bypass the legislature. In another formulation, Boyer said a legislature "cannot vest primary powers of legislation in any authority, including the electors, without providing for presentation of the legislation to the Lieutenant Governor for royal assent."

Boyer suggests, and we agree, that the Imperial decision against direct democracy was a ridiculous pretext which ignored what everyone knows to be the reality: the crown is a rubber stamp for the decisions of the legislators, whoever they may be. We think it is unlikely the Supreme Court of Canada will choose to disgrace itself or draw the monarchy into further disrepute when it takes up these questions.

FAIRNESS IN CITIZEN LAWMAKING

Some U.S. opponents of direct democracy suggest that the whole exercise is a chimera because the initiative campaigns have become a playground for the same political lobbyists, pollsters, direct mail fundraisers and advertising experts who play such a large part in regular electioneering for candidates and political parties. This is the same school of thought which holds that it takes only three things to win an election or a referendum: money, money and money. This isn't always true, as Canadian proponents of the Charlottetown Accord discovered last year when they spent $11.8 million on campaign advertising and the accord was defeated by opponents who spent $850,000. Still it is evident that in California an industry has grown up around the Initiative including the appearance of firms and individuals devoted, for a fee, to the collection of signatures and other consultants who put together entire campaigns. Since 1956 the 18 most expensive Initiative campaigns have involved outlays totalling $225 million and it is not uncommon for the opponents and proponents to spend a combined total of $1 million. Industries whose interests are in any way threatened — tobacco, insurance, liquor, nuclear — dig deep into corporate coffers to try to prevent unfavorable laws from going on the books. One nuclear energy campaign hit the $5 million mark, of which $4 million was spent by the industry, but the granddaddy of all was a 1988 showdown between insurance companies, consumer groups and trial lawyers over five different propositions in which the corporations spent $61 million and the total expenditure reached $80 million. There are still some inspiring examples of grassroots volunteer initiatives winning despite heavy spending by corporate opponents, but the role of big money is troubling. "The institutions of direct democracy were introduced into our system to effect a shift of power and a shift of influence in favor of causes whose adherents were numerous and passionate but not well-financed or well-connected," comments California law professor Daniel Lowenstein. His study concludes that "the power of some groups to raise enormous sums of money to oppose ballot propositions, without regard to any breadth or depth of popular feeling, seriously interferes with the ability of other groups to use the institutions of direct democracy as they were intended to be used."[28]

Cronin reports that corporate America has only a 25 per cent success rate in promoting its own pet projects through initiatives, but a 75 per cent success rate in defeating the initiatives of others in matters such as nuclear safety, mandatory bottle deposits, and reform of public utility regulations. The lopsided spending imbalances were endorsed in a U.S. Supreme Court decision which ruled that restrictions on corporate spending infringed freedom of speech, and by the Federal Communications Commission's abandonment in 1987 of its longstanding fairness doctrine. That regulatory rule had obliged television broadcasters to provide reasonably balanced coverage of controversial issues, including free-time opportunities for opponents to respond to paid television

---

28   Cited in Cronin, op. cit. p. 106

advertisements. The California Commission on Campaign Financing has urged that both U.S. courts and broadcast regulators reconsider in the interest of restraining "the corrosive and distorting effects of immense aggregations of wealth that are accumulated with the help of the corporate form and that have little or no correlation to the public's support for the corporation's political ideas."[29]

In Canada most of these questions have been addressed and resolved differently in the Canada Elections Act and particularly in the Elections Act of Quebec, the province where the issues of direct democracy have received the most intense scrutiny. These rules to organize and restrain campaign expenditures were in effect during the 1992 constitutional referendum and belong in a permanent Initiative and Referendum Act.

Umbrella Yes and No Committees. The chief electoral officer shall invite MPs and other citizens prominently associated with support for or opposition to a measure to form campaign committees and adopt a name and bylaws. The committee bylaws shall set the standards, conditions and formalities for affiliation and financing. All expenditures in connection with the vote must be reported to and authorized by one of the two committees. In Britain, where this was first done in 1975, the committees were called "Britain in Europe" and "National Referendum Campaign." In Quebec in 1980 they were named simply "Yes" and "No", and the 1992 Canada committees followed the same path.

Expenditure Limits and Financing. Each committee shall have an official agent and an auditor. Total expenditures per committee shall not exceed the equivalent of 50 cents per elector in 1993 dollars, about $8.5 million. Each committee shall make a complete statement of income and expense to the chief electoral officer, including the names of contributors giving more than $100. Contributions of more than $10,000 shall be reported within 48 hours, and the chief electoral officer shall make such information public.

---

29   Op. cit. p. 28

Political Broadcasting. The town hall meeting is gone but television is very much with us. An informed vote in this era requires television exposure guaranteed under the legal authority of the Canadian Radio-television and Telecommunications Commission for the arguments of the committees for and against any Initiative or Referendum, a principle that was recognized during Canada's constitutional vote in 1992. A 28-day free-time television campaign period shall be divided into two parts: a preliminary stage during which each committee is entitled to two minutes daily or the equivalent at times of its choosing on each television channel, and an intensive stage during which that is increased to four minutes daily or the equivalent. Between the two campaign stages, 14 to 21 days before the vote, there shall be a 60 minute debate between representatives of the two committees televised simultaneously on all channels. As recommended by the Lortie commission, parliamentary, public access and community cable channels shall broadcast the advertisements and the debate three times as often as the commercial broadcasters.

Mail subsidy. Canada Post shall deliver letter mail on behalf of the committees at a price no greater than the addressed third class bulk rate, or the unaddressed "admail" rate charged to its most preferred customer.

MINORITY RIGHTS

Direct lawmaking raises a fear that a majority of voters will on occasion fail to be respectful of racial, ethnic, religious or other minorities. The Charter of Rights provides significant protection in that regard, but the most important defence is and always will be the basic good sense of the Canadian people. It remains true that lawmakers and voters alike can make mistakes, as Parliament itself proved when it rode roughshod over civil rights during World War II by interning "enemy aliens" of Japanese ancestry. The long U.S. record of direct democracy indicates that the electorate's judgment is reasonably enlightened and we expect the Canadian electorate, when it becomes self-governing, to be at least as responsible.

5

OPEN DEMOCRATIC GOVERNMENT

IN THE LONG WAKE OF THE 1992 referendum a majority of Canadians including a large number of Quebecers will be grateful if their senior governments stop toying with the constitutional playdough and either do nothing or attend to something useful — the protection of the environment, the health of the economy, the training of the labor force or other such mundane matters.

Canadians of conservative persuasion still think we have too much government doing too many things and doing them badly. Most liberals and social democrats still believe government can be creative but have learned to be skeptical about expensive programs under centralized government control. The public's opposition to heavy taxation, and its resentment toward unresponsive and inefficient public bureaucracies, is too strong to be ignored and too persistent to be wrong.

What all Canadian democrats can surely agree on is that there will continue to be major disagreements about the proper mix of private and government activity, and all the other great questions of public policy, as long as there are living, breathing Canadians; that the balance of public opinion on any matter may shift from time to time; that it is the job of political parties to offer leadership and choices on the major issues; that a democratic Parliament should reflect and give expression to the public's verdicts; and that the public service of Canada should carry out Parliament's instructions with as much civility, sensitivity and efficiency as possible. This is not the way politics now works in Canada, and it is often not the way public bureaucracy works. We need a democracy which works better regardless of which set of politicians happens to be occupying the ministers' offices.

The most promising strategy for a new Democracy League trying to get democratic reform without relying on the good will of the established parties is schematically quite simple. First we must acquire the power of Initiative, and then we must use the Initiative to vote into effect a system of proportional representation in Parliament. That in turn will induce substantial changes in the way Parliament operates which will lead to improvements in the quality of Canadian democracy and government. Wherever Parliament continues to lag, we will use further Initiatives to set the agenda for the open, democratic government that the vast majority of Canadians wants.

The requirements of open government are no great mystery, although they are known to Canadians only in theory. The ideas are often discussed, and occasionally even promised in election campaigns, only to be swallowed and suffocated in the usual bog of majority government, pathological cabinet secrecy and furtive special interest lobbying.

REFORM OF THE HOUSE OF COMMONS

Idealists on Parliament Hill sometimes allow themselves to dream of a world not run by the party whips — a world in which a Member of Parliament might occasionally engage in an independent intelligent act. They imagine MPs from different parties working together in committees to research a problem, hold public hearings, and draft legislation which becomes the law of the land.

Peter Dobell of the Parliamentary Centre, working with financial assistance from the Donner Canadian Foundation, prepared and circulated what has turned out to be an influential discussion of that vision in 1992 as part of a larger project to find antidotes for Parliament's declining reputation. Many of Dobell's proposals were picked up by Kim Campbell and other Conservative leadership candidates, and Liberal leader Jean Chrétien also uses a couple of them as talking points. The difficulty, as Dobell acknowledged, is that the changes in parliamentary behavior he wants require a simultaneous change in attitude and practice by the government and opposition parties.

In our view the political parties can't and won't undergo any large change in attitude or adopt new tactics until the basic rules of the electoral game are changed. Dobell and his patrons at the Donner Foundation appear to share that assessment because it was they who first reacted to the Lortie commission's abdication of responsibility by encouraging Michael Cassidy's 1992 research into proportional representation for Canada. We assume, in the pages that follow, that the constructive ideas will not become reality until the House of Commons is elected by proportional representation and a new, more substantive and policy-oriented style of political competition is permitted to emerge in Canada.

Term of Parliament. One of the underlying reasons for cheap politicking and partisan bickering in Canadian politics is the perpetual threat of an election at the pleasure of the prime minister. The opposition must always be ready to fight at any moment the governing party finds opportune — an arrangement which leaves little room for trust between parties. A better procedure is the one used in New Zealand where the elections are held every three years on a fixed and predetermined schedule. To maintain responsible and effective government, however, there must be some allowance for deviation from the fixed term of office: it should be possible to dissolve Parliament and hold a general election if no party or coalition of parties is able to form a government.

Confidence Votes. Another source of partisan rigidity, gamesmanship and frenetic travelling by Canadian MPs is the notion that a defeat of any signficant government bill is automatically the defeat of the government and requires an election. The implications for party discipline when the government's majority is slim are obvious: it must be very, very tight. And in fact, the grip of the party whips is pervasive, reaching right down into every vote in every special and standing committtee, even when the government has a comfortable majority. As Benno Frisen, a B.C. Conservative MP, observed several years ago:

Experience has been that the longer a government is in office the more every vote is maybe not a vote of confidence but a vote of reputation, which is close to confidence, and therefore you have to have uniformity.[1]

The macho defence of reputation is so complete that majority governments routinely defeat opposition motions even when they are worded to conform exactly with government policy. In 1991, for example, Rey Pagtakhan (NDP-Winnipeg North) moved a motion declaring that "this House reaffirm its commitment to Medicare." Government House leader Harvie Andre interpreted it as an opposition challenge to the government's exclusive power to spend money and told Conservative MPs to vote against it even though, he said, the government remained committed to medicare. The solution to this problem is not complicated. All parties must agree that confidence in the government is at stake only when a motion explicitly says so. The German Bundestag takes this a step farther and specifies that a motion to defeat the government is not in order unless it also nominates the proposed head of the next government. If this became the standard approach in the Parliament of Canada, the rejection of a bill or even the reduction of parts of the government's spending estimates would mean just that and no more. The fate of the government would not always hang in the balance, and the rule of party whips would not need to be so oppressive.

This more relaxed approach to the confidence convention becomes essential in a Parliament in which no party has a majority, a likely result when many parties compete under British voting rules and a near-certain result under proportional representation voting rules. In those circumstances it is more difficult for a government to be constantly aware of how all MPs will vote, and it is impractical to imagine that the government must change or the country must have an election every time a government miscalcu-

---

1   Cited in Dobell, P., A Larger Role for the House of Commons, a manuscript of the Parliamentary Centre.

lates the mood of the House. Frequent elections are particularly pointless in a PR system if nothing has happened to produce a substantial shift in party voting support— the new Parliament will look much like the old one.

Election Mandate. Canadian governments will have to give up the conceit that a majority in Parliament gives them licence to do whatever they want. They'll also have to flush the theory, advanced by Brian Mulroney during his lengthy and self-justifying farewell, that a leader can be either effective or popular but not both. It wasn't obvious whether Mulroney was trying to say that all policies disliked by the electorate are good policies, or only that the electorate will not support good policies, but our former leader did make one thing perfectly clear: he is no democrat.

In the United Kingdom victorious parties claim only a mandate to implement their election platform and require their members to vote the party line on platform measures. When new problems arise the government consults widely, takes opposition views into account, and relaxes party discipline because it does not assume that it has a popular mandate.[2]

Committee Work. The House of Commons has an extensive committee structure which keeps MPs busy but acts as little more than a rubber stamp for government policy. A few committees have produced strong and thoughtful reports only to find their work largely ignored, while mistrustful ministers view the committees as places where the opposition seeks, as usual, to make trouble for the government.

Dobell suggests, and Kim Campbell seems to have agreed, that Parliamentary committees can be useful only if government asks them for advice on problems for which it hasn't already chosen a solution and sends along some budgetary guidelines to keep the members' creativity within acceptable limits. The Standing Committee on Consumer and Corporate Affairs, Dobell reports, recently handled a draft bill on employee rights in corporate bankruptcy

---

2   Ibid. p. 23

"in a completely non-partisan manner." The greatest advantage is that a committee's public hearings allow for the views of interested parties to be expressed on the public record and to be rebutted publicly by other interested parties and makes it possible to bring out different regional perspectives.

> From a minister's perspective advice offered by a committee based on public hearings can have several advantages. The public consultation will bring into the open concerns that in any case will have to be addressed. The committee can launch some trial balloons and test the reaction. To the extent the committee can develop a consensus the minister will — if he or she chooses to follow the advice offered — have a much easier time with legislation when it reaches the House. While the initial phase may take longer, the total time needed to secure passage of the legislation through the House may actually be shorter.[3]

In the case of a minority or coalition government, this style of consultation through committee would be the obvious way to craft legislation acceptable to the House.

Senior public servants may be disturbed by the idea of strong parliamentary committees. Normally they act as gatekeepers to cabinet, conducting private consultations with lobbyists and presenting the ministers with various options — until they retire early, take their public service pensions and use their insider knowledge as private lobbyists. With a stronger committee system, many more MPs would have an opportunity to take a positive role in making laws and the ministers would have another significant source of information.

Budgeting Rules and Costing of Bills. Many of Canada's fiscal and debt woes can be traced back, as we outlined in Chapter One, to biases in representative democracy which are exaggerated by British electoral rules — in particular the tendency to offer bribes to concentrated groups of voters and other policies of short term

---

3   Ibid. p. 27

benefit while obscuring information about the long-term costs and the incidence of the tax burden. For democracy to work properly the public needs good information, and near the top of the list is a systematic method to overcome the fiscal illusion fostered by our political parties for so long — that benefits can be created without costs. The government must provide detailed information on the expected costs and benefits, both direct and indirect, of each bill as it is introduced to Parliament. The statement should describe the anticipated effect on the federal budget over a 10-year period. To counteract the tendency to shovel benefits toward industries and their workers at the expense of the general taxpayer, the cost-benefit statement should identify the categories of people expected to benefit from the statute and the categories of people who would bear the resulting cost burden. Similarly, to restrain the election-cycle bias toward short-term benefits and deferred costs, the statement should set out when the benefits will emerge and when the costs are to be paid.

Rounding out this notion that the cards should be on the table and not up the government's sleeve, the annual budget should be presented on a fixed schedule and preceded by a series of televised committee hearings on the parliamentary channel at which major interest groups and associations and other members of the public present their advice to the minister of finance — and comment on each other. The budget should include, in addition to the usual direct expenditure and revenue estimates, a separate and detailed tax expenditure statement — an estimate of the revenue lost to the government through each of the special interest exemptions and loopholes which riddle the tax legislation and which have spawned a large, unproductive industry of tax accountants, lawyers and consultants. Such a regular, official description of the tax loophole ripoffs would in all likelihood galvanize a successful citizen Initiative campaign for income tax simplification and fairness along the lines advocated in 1990 by Liberal MP Dennis Mills in his book *The Single Tax*.

REFORM OF THE BUREAUCRACY

The modern state is big and, no matter how hard the neo-conservatives wish, it will remain big. Leviathan may be restrained but never banished because we need it in a thousand different ways. Our real task is to tame and civilize the beast to make it serve us better. The essential reforms, we repeat, are a Parliament immunized by proportional representation against capture by narrow interests, and the citizen Initiative. These, along with an independent judiciary, are the basic tools for democratic oversight of the state. Parliamentarians and citizens alike find it hard to exercise the necessary vigilance, however, when they are blindfolded. The bias toward secrecy in the Canadian system of government must be replaced with a presumption of openness.

Access to Information Law. Canada's rules for giving citizens a peek at the information and reports generated by government bureaucracies are at present little more than a bad joke. As *The Globe and Mail* recently reported, a question to the National Capital Commission about the cost of renovation and furnishings at 24 Sussex Drive was parried by a demand for $19,000 to cover the purported cost of copying the documents. The federal law and counterpart provincial legislation allow lengthy delays in response to requests and set out a host of exemptions which excuse public officials and ministers from providing citizens with information.

Ken Rubin, a independent researcher who has personally filed 3,000 of the 70,000 requests for information made under the act over the past 10 years, has had to make 400 complaints to the Information Commissioner and has been involved in 30 federal court actions in attempts to pry loose information the politicians and bureaucracy don't want to yield. "In over half my applications," says Rubin, "I have met with delays, denial and creative avoidance and I'm not the only one. There have been 7,600 complaints and over 400 federal court actions."[4]

---

4   Ken Rubin, My Ten Best Access Hits, *The Globe & Mail*, July 3, 1993

In 1986 Rubin found that the Prime Minister's Office had issued written instructions requiring public officials to clear with it the release of any information potentially embarrassing to Brian Mulroney or his office. On a less personal plane, the government won't let the public see polls conducted at public expense despite rulings that there is no valid reason to withhold them, prompting Information Commissioner John Grace to observe that his annual reports to Parliament "might as well be shipped to Mars" for all the difference they make. The government refuses to provide the Auditor General with documentation on the decision to assist PetroCanada in a multi-billion-dollar corporate takeover because to do so would jeopardize a sacred principle — cabinet secrecy.

The reasons offered by government officials for refusing information never include the obvious ones: covering the minister's *derrière*, concealing the sweetheart deal with friends of the governing party, and the like. Instead we hear pious pleadings about the protection of national security, individual privacy, privileged communication, and commercially sensitive information. The information gathered and created at public expense by federal departments and agencies is still treated in large measure as the private property of the government of the day, which is to say the private property of the prime minister. The mentality is feudal in origin and remains almost untouched by the spread of democracy in modern societies over the past 200 years.

A new freedom of information law for Canada should specify that government information belongs to the taxpayers and must be provided or made readily available at reasonable cost unless the Information Commissioner rules the release is contrary to the public interest. The Information Commissioner should be appointed by and report to a parliamentary committee composed of equal numbers of representatives from each political party in the House of Commons. The commissioner should have the authority to impose penalties including suspension and dismissal on federal employees who obstruct the public's access to information without adequate justification. Federal employees will welcome the opportunity to serve the public as well as the government of the day.

Registration of Lobbyists. The business of government is vast and touches nearly every aspect of life. Interest groups of every kind and description try to exert influence on government decisions, either to gain advantage or to prevent unwanted state intrusion in their affairs. The most adept operate in teams capable of maintaining contact at all levels of the state and government apparatus. Access to the prime minister, the ministers and deputy ministers is always useful but some of the most successful lobbyists find it very effective to influence the bureaucracy at the level of policy analysts, directors and directors general where proposals to cabinet originate and potentially damaging impulses can be reshaped or nipped in the bud. The legitimate lobbyist's tools are reliable information, patience, persistence and persuasiveness. The old hands say a successful lobby is like a perfect crime: when it is done properly nobody even knows it has taken place.

As the special interests spend large amounts of time and money to influence decisions they pose two potential problems: corrupt practices, and decisions detrimental to unrepresented interests, especially the diffuse interests of the general taxpayer, the consumer or the natural environment. The only practical safeguard is to demand that lobbyists give notice of their activity so other affected interests may be alerted and make their voices heard.

At present Ottawa does make paid lobbyists register and indicate, in very broad terms, what subject matters they are working on, but so little is required that the registry prov_des no real clue to what's happening. Lobbyists working through coalitions or retained by lawyers should be required to disclose the identity of their ultimate patrons and the fees they pay, the specific nature of the projects on which they are engaged, the targets of their efforts, and their expenditures on each lobbying project. The lobbyists should also be required to report the history of their paid positions in political parties, ministers' offices or the public service of federal, provincial or municipal governments and their financial contributions to political parties.

One former lobbyist, Bill Eggertson, recently challenged the exclusive focus on lobbyists by asking why they should be blamed for lousy decisions by politicians:

> When a maintenance contract for CF-18 aircraft was not awarded to Winnipeg despite the superior qualifications of Bristol Aerospace, I didn't blame the lobbyist who was paid to extol the virtues of job creation in Montreal where Canadair got the contract. My criticism was reserved for politicians who overturned the recommendations of their own experts and capitulated to the flawed arguments. When millions of dollars are squandered in a minister's riding, I don't censure the consultant who wrote the proposal; I condemn the public officials who fail to provide basic accountability for the management of our country.... What is urgently needed is to oblige our politicians and public officials to tell us with whom they are wheeling and dealing — to list, in a public registry, the private interests they meet.... The onus for proper government must be placed squarely on public office-holders.[5]

The registry which Eggerton suggests could be the official day books of every minister and designated senior public officials, the list to be determined by the same parliamentary committee which oversees freedom of information. These public officials could be required by law to note the occurrence of meetings and substantive conversations with private interests about public business, and the day books could be open to public scrutiny. That, combined with the lobbyist register, would make the government of Canada's operations considerably more transparent than they now are.

Appointments. A raft of public positions such as citizenship court judge, immigration and refugee appeal board member, human rights commission, parole board and unemployment in-

---

5   "Keeping an Eye on Ottawa's Deals," *The Globe & Mail,* June 29, 1993

surance referee, are frequently used as patronage rewards for faithful members of the government party without much attention to the quality of work performance.[6] These positions should instead be allocated by the civil service commission to applicants on the basis of qualifications and merit. Appointments to major policy-making positions, such as Governor of the Bank of Canada or Chair of the Canadian Broadcasting Corporation, the National Transportation Agency, or the Canadian Radio-television and Telecommunications Commission, should be contingent on public hearings and confirmation by a committee of the House of Commons.

Ombudsman. Despite calls from the Canadian Bar Association, the Canadian Provincial Ombudsmen, the Law Reform Commission of Canada and others over the past 15 years, the government of Canada still has no Ombudsman. The function of trying to ensure fair treatment of Canadians by public officials is performed, after a fashion, by Members of Parliament. Refugees facing deportation making appeals to the immigration minister for compassion, the ill pleading for disability cheques from the Canada Pension Plan, seniors missing Old Age Security payments, and small business operators being squeezed by their banker or Revenue Canada all look to the MPs for assistance — if they can catch up with them.

Some Members of Parliament try to make themselves easily available to constituents and spend a large chunk of their $160,000 annual budget to maintain and staff a well-located constituency office. Others spend more time in Ottawa and avoid constituency service by requiring appointments booked well in advance. There is, says Metro Toronto MP Dennis Mills, no necessary connection between constituency service and re-election. "Senator (Keith) Davey and (former chief Liberal pollster) Marty Goldfarb told me I was crazy when they saw the big constituency

---

6   Immigrants are asked to name three Canadian political parties and in many citizenship courts there are only three correct answers — Liberal, Progressive Conservative and New Democrat.

office I was running," Mills recalls. "They said voters don't respect an MP who works hard for them." The senior Liberals told Mills about another MP who was working himself to death serving constituents in the belief that he was building the Liberal vote. Goldfarb asked for the names of 100 sure-fire Liberal voters from the MP's casework files, surveyed them and reported back that eight of every ten said they wouldn't support him. "But I solved their problems," said the astounded member. "They remember you took four days to return a phone call," said Goldfarb. Mills had a similar revelation when, at the instigation of a married couple with young children, he mobilized the entire Metro Liberal caucus to block the parole of a sex offender. "We put a lot of work into that, we kept the guy in jail, and the next time I saw that woman she was putting up posters in store windows for the National Party," Mills recalls. "I said I was shocked, and she wondered why. It makes you think that if you work too hard you'll work yourself right out of office."

Research for the Lortie Commission showed that the personal vote is not a large factor in Canadian politics, and that the turnover of MPs is high. Proportional representation, which offers the promise of major improvements in the way Parliament makes law, cannot and does not pretend to provide voters with elected local caseworkers. Clearly, when Canada adopts proportional representation, it will be necessary to establish a federal Ombudsman service. In fact, Prime Minister Kim Campbell has said such a service should be created now. She began developing the proposal while she was minister of justice and is convinced "that there could be a very positive role for a federal ombudsman office which could coordinate and strengthen similar existing federal resources and support departments and agencies of government in developing their own independent, effective commitment to fairness and service to the public."

Campbell said during her leadership campaign that what is needed is not "another burgeoning layer of federal bureaucracy" but rather "someone in government whose job it is to support citizens...in their dealings with an increasingly sophisticated and complex public bureaucracy.... It is now virtually impossible for a government minister, let alone a busy Member of Parliament or individual citizen, to possess the knowledge and expertise that is needed to effectively deal with every facet of the federal government." She said an executive within each federal department and agency should be designated to work with the Ombudsman to develop "systems for enhancing excellence in the delivery of service." We suggest that if the Ombudsman's staff is to be small but effective then the authority of the office to impose its rulings will have to be substantial.

Charter Challenges. Canada's Charter of Rights and Freedoms has produced important changes in the attitudes of Canadians but its impact will become skewed toward the protection of the privileged unless legal issues important to Canadians of modest means are regularily brought before the courts. The cancellation of the federal program to provide financial assistance for charter challenges to the laws of Canada was one economy measure that Canadian democracy simply cannot afford.

POLITICAL PARTY FINANCING REFORM

Perhaps the most amazing aspect of the financing of politics in Canada is just how little money it takes to gain control of the Canadian state. Federal program spending exceeds $120 billion each year and total spending is over $150 billion but the three federal parties which contend for the right to manage it take in a combined total of only $30 million in off-years and $60 million in an election year — an average of about $35 million a year. Putting aside the question of quality, the total annual cost of party representation is the equivalent of a levy of $2 per registered voter. It's a surprisingly small amount although, given a choice at this point, most Canadians would probably prefer two cups of coffee.

TABLE 5.1
Revenues of the Major Federal Parties
(millions of dollars)

	PC	Liberal	NDP
1985	15.1	6.2	6.5
1986	15.6	10.7	7.0
1987	13.1	8.9	6.8
1988	25.2	16.4	12.2
Reimbursement	1.8	1.5	1.6
1989	14.5	6.4	7.7
1990	11.3	13.8	9.0

Source: Adapted from the Lortie commission, *Reforming Electoral Democracy*, Vol. 1, p. 304

The national parties with their small memberships have great difficulty raising even these modest sums. The Liberal party accumulated a deficit of $5 million between 1980 and 1990, while the NDP went $2.5 million into the red over the same period. Only the Progressive Conservatives, by far the most effective fundraisers, were able to show a slight surplus of $1.25 million.

Party income depends on contributions from private sources, direct reimbursements of election expenses from the public purse and, increasingly, franchise fees or levies on riding associations which are often in better shape financially than the national party. The Conservatives raise 40 to 50 per cent of their revenue from individual contributions and 50 to 60 per cent from business organizations. The Liberals have been getting around 40 per cent from individuals and 60 per cent from business, while the New Democrats get 70 to 80 per cent from individuals and 15 to 25 per cent from trade unions.

In 1988, the last election year, only 313,000 individual Canadians made direct contributions to political parties — fewer than 2 per cent of the electors. The Conservatives received an average of $199 dollars from 53,900 people, the Liberals an average of $163 from 30,600 people, and the NDP an average of $69 from 118,400 people.

Here we must bear in mind that the taxpayer is paying most of the freight because most of the individual contributors claim tax credits and corporate donors write off their contributions as expenses of doing business. The political tax credit returns $75 of the first $100 contributed by an individual to a party, and political contributions all the way up to $1,150 get better tax treatment than donations to charities. The political tax credits claimed by individual Canadians in recent years have equalled about 30 per cent of total political party revenues.[7]

In fact, the Lortie commission reports, all direct and indirect taxpayer support of the national political parties costs $1 per voter per year. In other words, although most Canadians have no voice or influence in a political party, we are already supplying half their revenue on the basis of choices made by the parties themselves (election spending reimbursements), by executives of corporations (which claim tax deductions), and by a handful of individual contributors (who claim tax credits).[8]

This is a perverse system of public political funding which should be replaced by one which links political parties more directly to the voters they purport to represent. It is we, the voters of Canada, who should decide as we mark our ballots how public funds will be allotted to the political parties. Such systems are already in place in Quebec, New Brunswick and Prince Edward Island, and the same has been proposed for Canada by the Lortie commission and rejected by the House of Commons.

---

7   Lortie et al., *Reforming Electoral Democracy*, Vol. 1, p. 312
8   The tax credit system discriminates blatantly in favour of Canadians who pay income taxes. To give all low-income Canadians an equal opportunity to support a political party the tax credit would have to be refundable.

Lortie said that, instead of parties and candidates being reimbursed for election expenses, they should be paid for winning votes. The figure he proposed was $1.60 per vote, with the national party receiving $.60 and the local riding association $1. Lortie also examined suggestions that the political tax credit be strengthened as a further incentive to private contributions, but he quite properly rejected the idea. It is difficult to imagine giving a small number of individuals more leverage on the public purse when they are already permitted to spend as much as $3 of public funds for each $1 they put up themselves.

We think Lortie was on the right track but too timid in his critique of the public funding mechanisms. Voters should guide the allocation of public funds to parties, but the general rule should be that each voter carries equal weight in the allocation. Reimbursement for election expenses should be abolished at both the national and riding level, and so should the tax credits to individuals and tax deductions for corporations who give to the national political parties. In their place, the treasury should distribute the same total sum of money to the national parties in the form of a public allowance of $1 a year for each vote received at the last general election. Based on 1988 results this would have provided the national Conservative party over the past five years with $5.7 million a year, the national Liberal party $4.2 million, the NDP $2.7 million, Reform $275,000, the Rhinos $52,000, the Greens $47,000, and so on down the list.

The political tax credit must be retained to deal with four political fundraising situations which can't be completely handled by the pay-per-vote regime just described: riding level campaigns; registered political parties before their first general election; nomination contests in registered political parties; and leadership contests in registered political parties. In all these circumstances the public has its usual interest in encouraging fair competition, and there is no way better than the tax credit to accomplish the purpose. The riding candidates, as Lortie suggested, should be paid $1 per vote from public funds after the election campaign. However a restricted version of the tax credit, perhaps the current 75 per cent credit for contributions up to $100, should be retained to keep the door open for mavericks with grassroots support whether as independents or under a party label.

Under this proposal for public financing of political parties, private contributions unassisted by the taxpayer are still permitted in nomination contests, in leadership contests, to riding associations and to national parties. However, as Lortie argued, the infusion of substantial public funds into political parties changes their character and duties. They are no longer simply private associations for the pursuit of power, but instruments of public policy. In return for public funds they must be required by law to adopt codes of ethical practice, to file their constitutions with the chief electoral officer, to set spending limits for nominations and leadership contests, and to require full financial disclosure from candidates in those contests prior to the votes. Similarly the riding associations and national parties must be required to make financial disclosures prior to a general election.

The entire system of financial disclosure and compliance with spending limits should be overseen by a new Canada Elections Commission, but its membership should not be restricted to House of Commons parties. The commission, which will have authority to prosecute violations of the Elections Act, should be composed of one representative from each registered political party, a judge of the federal court, the Canada elections commissioner and the chief electoral officer.

The consequences of switching to pay-per-vote public funding will be positive under any voting rules. The public monies, until now monopolized by the Liberals, Conservatives and NDP, will be spread further and give other parties a better chance to be heard. Under the combination of proportional representation voting and pay-per-vote financing not only will smaller parties be heard during the election campaign but voting for them will no longer be an act of existential protest or desperation. Fair voting and fair party financing rules will move us toward a more vigorous, effective democracy in which policies count, parties strive to keep faith with their voters, and all significant currents of opinion are represented. The resulting Parliament will, we think, be disposed to enact the kinds of open government reforms described here and others that surely will be proposed as more Canadians realize it is possible to move politics beyond the familiar, dreary rivalries of the established parties. If a new multi-party Parliament can't muster a majority for change in important matters, then we may expect some parties within it to organize Initiatives to give all Canadians the last word on how the public's business should be done.

We voters have been berated by Kim Campbell for our apathy and collective failure to join established political parties. In reply we should offer the prime minister a challenge : adopt our reforms and make the political parties worth joining. We should also issue a warning: when we get organized to join the Progressive Conservative Party, the Liberal Party and the New Democratic Party *en masse,* it won't be to promote the greater glory of the leaders.

Senate Reform. No discussion of the Canadian system of government is complete without a nod to the second chamber, the place where so many friends of the governing party have found, as *Maclean's* editor Bob Lewis neatly put it, "a taskless thanks." The decisive moment in the 1984 campaign which brought Brian Mulroney to office was, by most accounts, his televised attack on Liberal leader John Turner for a raft of patronage appointments. Mulroney promised a new order and Canadians wanted a new order. Nine years later it's all as bad as before or worse, and Mulroney has left office in an orgy of patronage appointments including lifetime Senate sinecures for key party bagmen and the patronage coordinator, Marjory LeBreton. Unlike Senator Pat Carney, who wants to be loved and respected, most senators are content to be ignored and most Canadians have been content to ignore them. But every now and again, as during the recent attempt by the appointees to scoop an extra $6,000 a year each in tax-free allowances from the treasury, we are prompted to ask why we must support these partisans.

In Britain the House of Lords functioned as a chamber of sober second thought which could if necessary overrule the dangerous democratic passions of the lower orders in the House of Commons. In Canada, where democratic passions in the House are pretty much unknown, the function has mutated and the Senate's role is to act as a check upon the unbridled power of the prime minister. Twice in recent times, during the free trade debate and the goods and services tax dispute, the Senate has tried to obstruct legislation. In the first case it forced an election. In the second, the net result was Mulroney's appointment of eight extra Senators to create a Tory majority in the Senate.

The democratic reforms proposed in this book make the Senate irrelevant and unnecessary. A proportional representation House of Commons is unlikely to throw up the one-party tyrannies which appear so regularly under British voting rules. If by chance a coalition government attempted to proceed with a controversial policy such as free trade or the GST without establishing a broad consensus, the opposition parties and popular movements would have a democratic defence in the Initiative. Furthermore, our proposals for public financing of political parties on a pay-by-vote system should greatly reduce the need for party bagpersons, and thus for their Ottawa retirement home.[9]

There remains the argument from some Canadians that a Triple E senate — elected, equal and effective — is needed to protect regional interests. Regional differences are already represented and cultivated by provincial governments to the point that the Canadian state is in danger of disintegration. But whatever the merits of the Triple E campaign in the present context, many of its objectives will be addressed by switching the House of Commons to proportional representation. A PR House of Commons will harbor several national parties with members from every region so the regions will always be represented on the government side. If a national government somehow contrives policies genuinely repug-

---

9   As Frank Stronach suggests in the foreword, it would be possible instead of abolishing the partisan Senate to replace it with another group of citizens to act as a restraint on the prime minister and the majority of the House of Commons. He suggests a form of sortition, or selection by lot, supplemented by elections with little campaigning and no overt party organization. Our approach has not been to try to get rid of political parties but to propose rules which will allow them to serve democracy better.

nant or harmful to the people of an entire region, whether Quebec, the West, Ontario or the Atlantic, the region's voters will support regional parties like the Bloc Québécois and Reform in numbers which will make them impossible to ignore.

Let us declare our bias as explicitly as possible. Any constitutional formulation which tries to provide representation to trees, or barrels of oil, or bushels of wheat, or cod fish (if any can be found), is misguided. Any formulation which tries to invest Prince Edward Island with powers equal to Ontario, or for that matter Quebec with powers equal to the rest of Canada, flies in the face of common sense. The only principle which will stand the test of time is that all Canadians are equals, and each vote is of equal weight. Our politics should consist of uniting like-minded Canadians from every region in political parties to advance the common good as they understand it.

6

TELEDEMOCRACY:
OPENING THE CHANNELS

*The broadcasting system should be
"varied and comprehensive and should provide
reasonable, balanced opportunity for the expression
of differing views on matters of public concern."*

— The Broadcasting Act, 1978

*During an election period a licensee
shall allocate time for the broadcasting of
programs, advertisements or announcements
of a partisan political character on an equitable basis
to all accredited political parties and rival candidates.*

— Television Broadcasting Regulations, 1987

*Freedom of expression in the electoral process
cannot be achieved unless the laws
that govern this process explicitly
seek to promote fairness.*

— Pierre Lortie, 1991

THIS FALL MOST OF US want to see the party leaders debate on television — but just which leaders? Campbell, Chrétien and McLaughlin will be there, of course, and so should Lucien Bouchard of the Bloc Québécois and Preston Manning of the Reform Party. No debate would be complete without them. And what about Mel Hurtig of the National Party or Chris Lea of the Green Party? Why should they be left out?

The debates are the best chance we get to size up the major party leaders and see how they deal with each other. Many of us also want to see how some of the alternative party leaders look on a national platform. If we were voting under proportional representation rules, hearing from the small parties would help us understand their priorities, what terms they might set for supporting a government, and which other parties they think they can work with in Parliament. But even in this 1993 general election, with any luck our last under British voting rules, we will certainly give places in the House of Commons to more than three parties. We'll also find it more necessary than usual to understand what the small parties are saying and why their vote is on the rise.

Full-blown leaders' debates should be our right, especially when the Canada Elections Act, between the last election and the end of this one, will have required us as taxpayers to support the political parties to the tune of more than $100 million. But the parties have not accepted any obligation in return for this conscripted largesse. The leaders' debates, so central to our modern politics, are not required by law. They take place at the discretion of and on terms set by the major party leaders and the television networks.

If Kim Campbell, Jean Chrétien and Audrey McLaughlin want to debate Lucien Bouchard, or feel they don't dare avoid him, Bouchard is allowed to debate. If one of the major party leaders objects, either Bouchard doesn't debate or there is no debate. The same goes for Preston Manning. As we finished writing in August the television networks had given the party leaders a backroom ultimatum: Bouchard and Manning were to be allowed on, or there would be no national televised debates.

The threat by the networks, like much else in the process, was unprincipled. They didn't state there would be a debate with Manning and Bouchard and leave the major party leaders to join in or stay out as they chose. That would involve political risk, to which our state-licensed broadcasters are averse. Rather than incur the displeasure of a potential prime minister, the networks bravely offered to sacrifice the public's interest — the debate itself.

The ploy, we admit, was unlikely to fail. Jean Chrétien and Audrey McLaughlin as challengers had already declared their willingness to debate. Prime Minister Kim Campbell, heading a party low in the polls and herself a champion of inclusive politics, could not refuse without suffering a massive loss of credibility. But in such matters nothing proceeds quickly. There was a proposal for one "town hall" pre-writ television encounter in early September but the networks and the major parties kept the wraps on what sort of debating would take place during the actual campaign. Would there be debates, and how many? If Bouchard debated for French-speaking audiences, would he also join the English-speaking programs? Would French-speaking audiences hear Manning? And what about Hurtig and the leaders of other alternative parties? Our bet was that the networks, three established parties and the two muscular regional interlopers would try to keep Hurtig, Lea and others off the debates. The other possibility was that Kim Campbell would read her polling data and embarrass Chrétien by proposing they debate both Hurtig and Lea, two party leaders capable of siphoning off Liberal votes the same way the Reform Party has sapped Conservative support.

The months of backroom jockeying over the 1993 debate format underline the ongoing absurdity of leaving such decisions to the prime minister, the opposition leader and the networks. The uncertain status of televised debates is only the most glaring symptom of pervasive weaknesses in our teledemocracy which we should no longer tolerate. As the Lortie royal commission said:

> Any examination of fairness in electoral competition, of campaign costs or of public confidence in the electoral process must come to terms with the central role of the modern mass media.... Virtually

every aspect of the election campaign will involve the media; in fact, to a large degree the media are the stage on which the election is fought.[1]

Lortie observes that unregulated political competition through the mass media is always unfair because parties with superior access to money can, through saturation advertising, dominate all other voices. Permitting uncontrolled political competition through the mass media, as one of the commission's studies put it, makes no more sense than allowing every private citizen who can afford one to keep a standing army.

The royal commission devoted special attention to broadcast media because of their intrusive reach into every Canadian home, their inherent capacity to command the attention of passive viewers, their known influence on young and undecided voters and their dominant role in electoral politics. Declining newspaper readership and the relative credibility and perceived impact of television have for the past three decades made it the preferred channel for waging national campaigns. Party strategists choose television over other media not only for audience size but also for its greater emotional impact and ability to persuade.[2] These realities led Lortie and his colleagues to warn against any thought of deregulating television use during elections.

> The closer broadcast regulations are to creating a free market, the greater the likely imbalance in media access among opposing candidates.... Fairness in electoral competition requires that the contenders be given reasonable access to the media channels that are likely to be most effective in carrying their arguments to voters.

The commission's thinking builds on a Canadian tradition which, from the earliest days of radio in the 1930s, has favored a system of regulated broadcast competition among recognized

---

1   RC Vol. 1, p. 374
2   Kline, Stephen et al, Political Advertising in Canada, RC Research, Vol. 21, p. 230

political parties through alotments of free broadcast time. Since 1974 that tradition has been overwhelmed by a newer regime of paid broadcast advertising combined with public funding of political parties. The intimate link between public funding and paid advertising is shown in the 1988 party election expense reports: election advertising accounted for nearly 60 per cent of all spending by the Liberal and Progressive Conservative parties and nearly 50 per cent of the total NDP expenditure, and television consumed the lion's share of all three advertising budgets.

According to the Lortie commission's opinion surveys, only 22 per cent of Canadians favor a no-holds-barred American approach to campaign spending while 75 per cent support spending limits.[3]

What most Canadians do not appreciate is the extent to which the NDP, Liberal and Conservative parties, flying under cover of the electorate's desire for fairness and spending restraint, have manipulated the Canada Elections Act to favor themselves at the expense of the public interest. In times past parties in goverment redrew electoral boundaries to squeeze partisan advantage from a constituency-based voting system. In the age of radio and television the three major parties have colluded in a modern perversion of democracy: television gerrymandering. Among them they have rigged the allocation of public funding and broadcast time to confer permanent advantage on themselves, kneecap potential competitors, and petrify the party structure of the House of Commons forever in its present form.

The basic deal to finance Liberal, Progressive Conservative and NDP television advertising expenses from public funds was welded into the Canada Elections Act in 1974. Its effects linger and grow so that this fall, unless the courts intervene, our television screens will be chock-a-block with ads for the three par-

---

3   RC Vol. 1. p. 388. The respondents were asked which of the two following statements came closest to their view. "Freedom of speech is such a fundamental right that parties should be allowed to advertise as much as they wish" or "We should limit spending on party advertising, otherwise parties with more money will have an unfair advantage."

ties with very little heard from any other party, even Reform and the National party which have money to spend on broadcast advertising. The law as written by the Liberals, Conservatives and New Democrats doesn't allow them to spend it.

Television offers three different ways for politicians to reach voters: news and public affairs coverage, in which they get exposure but must endure the interpretations, filtering and comments of journalists; leaders debates and interview programs, in which the access to voters is much less filtered; and political time, paid and free, in which the politicians are in complete control of the message. All three types of exposure are important. The first two are handled by informal understandings between the parties and the TV networks while the last — paid time and free time — is controlled by the Canada Elections Act.

TELEVISION GERRYMANDERING

All television networks or stations are required to set aside 390 minutes of prime time during the last four weeks of an election campaign for paid political advertising by parties. The networks also donate time, not necessarily prime, for the free use of political parties during the same period. CBC English, CBC French and CTV offer 214 minutes while TVA and Quatre Saisons offer 62 minutes. On the radio networks the English and French CBC-AM offer 120 minutes, while Radiomutuel and Télémedia offer 62 minutes.

The law spells out who is allowed to buy paid political time and the free time is handed out in the same proportions. Here's how the English-language allocation for this year's election looked when it was first worked out in 1991.

Table 6.1
Allowed Paid TV Advertising Time

Party	Minutes
Progressive Conservative	173
Liberal	110
New Democrat	71
Reform	10
Christian Heritage	7
Rhinoceros	7
Green	7
Commonwealth	5
Communist	0
Libertarian	0
Confederation of Regions	0
Social Credit	0
Total	390

The Broadcasting Act says the allocation of time for partisan broadcasts must be equitable, but the House of Commons parties have mocked that standard by their twisting of the Canada Elections Act. As the table shows they've authorized themselves to hog nearly 95 per cent of all available radio and television political advertising time during elections. They've done it by requiring that time be allocated on the basis of factors only a House of Commons party can meet under British voting rules: seats won at the last election and votes won at the last election. Only one-fifth of the index has been based on yet another retrospective factor, the number of constituencies contested at the last election, which gives other parties a small opening to get into the game.

The significance of this gerrymander shouldn't be underestimated. As the Lortie commission observed:

Paid time is important in federal elections, given the high level of volatility in the Canadian electorate and the effectiveness of paid time in reaching undecided voters. Over the last five elections, an average of approximately 43 per cent of Canadian voters made their voting decisions during the campaign, responding mainly to the issues of that campaign rather than to longer-term ideological or partisan commitments. Volatility was particularly high in 1988. One survey indicated that...more than 60 per cent of voters reported making their vote decisions during the campaign itself...and 25 per cent of voters stated that they had changed their voting intentions at least once during the campaign.[4]

The 1988 Canadian National Election Study concluded that there were significant shifts in voting intention during the campaign period in eight of the last ten federal elections. Party professionals, based on their own polling observations during the campaigns, have no doubt that it is television broadcasts which move the numbers. The established parties are no longer able to inspire much voter loyalty but they have perpetuated themselves by using the law to enforce a three-party propaganda cartel.

Political advertisements, although many voters view them with suspicion, have a significant influence on some others. U.S. research indicates that many voters learn more about policy issues from party advertisements than from news coverage. Recent studies in Canada also suggest that many voters, especially those who don't follow politics closely, become aware of issues and party positions and form impressions of the leaders from party advertisements. The attention-grabbing and repetitive nature of advertising does promote learning, the Lortie commission noted.

Most of the 1988 party advertisements had at least some policy content, and the most effective of them distilled a central policy argument. Although the points were made dramatically and not argued in detail, the outlines of the debate were presented in the paid time.

---

4   RC Vol. 1, p. 384

Interested voters, having learned of the competing positions, could turn to other sources for further information.[5]

This is why parties are willing to spend $100,000 per minute for full exposure on the entire Canadian broadcast system and proportionate amounts for sub-campaigns tailored and targeted to regions and selected swing constituencies. It's also the reason that in most countries paid political television advertising is banned or closely regulated. France, the United Kingdom and Sweden, for example, provide parties with free time only. Elsewhere, only the United States places no limits on the amount of advertising time that may be purchased. In Germany's last election the two largest parties were allowed 25 minutes of paid time each and the smaller parties 12.5 minutes. The Australian government, after a two-year deregulation experiment during which the cost of political advertising soared, passed a law in 1991 banning paid time altogether.

"In many democracies," observed Lortie, "the issues of controlling election advertising costs and of appropriate rules for paid time for political parties have been matters of concern in recent years."[6] The Canadian rules, he said, are unfair — by which he appears to mean unconstitutional.

The effect of this allocation, should an election be called under the existing rules, is to place an upper limit of [ten] minutes on the amount of time that can be bought from any broadcaster by any party other than the three largest parties. Since broadcasters are forbidden to sell more...this allocation would not allow any smaller party to run an effective advertising campaign regardless of its capacity to raise funds. Although such a party could buy as much print advertising as it could afford, it would not be able to compete on television or radio, the most potent instruments of modern election campaigns. The unfairness of the existing system lies not only

---

5   Ibid. p. 384
6   Ibid. p. 385

in the imbalance shown but also in its clear bias against emerging parties, regardless of popular support and resources....[7]

Lortie went on to recommend new rules to regulate political broadcasting but this part of his report was completely ignored by the House of Commons parties. Their unfair election law, condemned by their own partisans on the royal commission, will once again control and distort communications in a Canadian election campaign.

FREE POLITICAL TIME

Canadians believed, long before the Charter of Rights and Freedoms lent precision to our sense of rights, that equal opportunity for political communication is valuable to our democracy. Thus, in the early days of radio, Prime Minister Mackenzie King suggested to Parliament that there should be a free-time allocation.

> Radio...plays such an important part in all matters affecting public opinion that it would be quite proper that some provision be made whereby, for example, each political party which has a representative following should be entitled to have broadcast at the expense of the state one or two addresses which would set forth its platform or policies before the people.... I think there ought to be some definite understanding that radio ... will be used in a manner which will not give to one party which may happen to have more in the way of financial backing than other parties a larger use of that national instrument.[8]

The Canadian Broadcasting Corporation later set aside an hour a week year-round for party programming on its own stations. When the format was transferred to television it appeared for many years as the political "talking heads" whose main impact was to en-

---

7   Ibid. p. 387
8   Speaking to the House of Commons in 1934. Cited by Trudel, P., in The Legal and Constitutional Framework for Regulating Election Campaign Broadcasting, RC Research Vol. 21, p. 110

courage the deft use of remote control channel changers. By 1988 the major political parties had stopped trying to use free time as it was originally intended — for longer discourses on political questions. They chopped up the alloted 214 minutes into one and two-minute segments, kept 85 per cent of it for themselves, and treated it as free commercial time. The smaller parties with their tiny allotments — most got only four minutes — had no choice but to do the same.

This baldly inequitable scheme does not reflect the will or the democratic spirit of Canadians. Lortie confirmed through his surveys that we want a lot more direct communication between politicians and voters than we've been getting. "This appears to be a major consideration in the public support for mandatory leadership debates and in the general support for other unmediated sources [of political information]. In addition, there is widespread sentiment that the system should be more open to small parties," Lortie said. With one eye on the Charter of Rights — and the kinds of strict court orders for allocation of television exposure it could inspire — he advised the established parties to rethink the wisdom of the lopsided time allocations.

> A free-time system that provides meaningful access for smaller parties appears to us to be the best alternative to intrusive regulations. The provision of alternative forms of direct access to national audiences promotes fairness and diversity in electoral communication without raising concerns about traditional media freedoms.[9]

The royal commissioners reached for inspiration to the extensive free-time tradition of other countries, particularly the proportional representation democracies in which a diversity of political expression is considered healthy. Of the nine countries the commission studied most closely, only the United States makes no provision for free-time broadcasts by political parties.

---

9   Ibid. p. 399

Even there, Lortie reports, various proposals for party free time, debate and issues programs are circulating as friends of democracy try to find ways "to provide more substantive information to citizens and thus counter growing cynicism about electoral politics."[10]

Australia, Denmark, France, Germany, the United Kingdom, Israel, Norway and Sweden all make provision for free political broadcast time. Denmark gives equal television time to any party that collects signatures equal in number to the votes required at the last election to win one seat in the legislature. The equivalent figure for Canada would be 44,000 signatures. There are eight parties represented in the Danish Folketing. Australia allocates time to parties which contest at least 10 seats and show evidence of popular support. The time consists of two-minute slots plus a full broadcast of the leader's policy speech at the start of the campaign. Norway gives equal time if a party has been previously represented in the Storting and runs candidates in a majority of districts. There are six parties with elected members. Sweden similarly gives equal television access to the six parties represented in the Riksdag.

In the United Kingdom the time is alloted equally among the three largest parties and to the regional parties in proportion to their vote at the last election. In Germany the two-and-a-half minute spots which run immediately before or after prime time news are allowed in proportion to the vote at the last election. Israel's public broadcaster, which must accommodate 16 parties, schedules a 30 minute program each evening before the 9 p.m. news within which slots up to 10 minutes in length are alloted in proportion to the vote at the last election. The format generates "lively debate," Lortie reports, as parties often use their time to deal with issues raised by other parties in previous segments. The example was sufficiently compelling to persuade the royal com-

---

10   Ibid. p. 403

mission to make it the centrepiece of its free time recommendations.

Lortie said the English language networks and broadcasters should be required to provide ten 30-minute program time slots and French networks five 30-minute slots with at least 24 minutes in each for the political parties during an election campaign. [He did not explain why our election laws assume French-speaking voters need less information than others. Are they all switching to English channels just to watch political commercials?]. He suggested a magazine format with party segments in four-minute units and a frequency of two programs per week "to be broadcast simultaneously by all participating broadcasters."

> To grasp the possible benefits of the free-time proposal it is helpful to imagine what the political parties might do with their segments. The early broadcasts might feature the leaders of the largest parties, as is done in Great Britain and Australia. The leaders of the smaller parties could respond or use their segments to focus on a competing set of issues. Standard features, like profiles of party leaders and other prominent candidates, could be supplemented by other creative materials that highlighted differences among the parties or drew attention to particular strengths and weaknesses. More simply, parties could present highlights of their leaders' campaign speeches, providing the substance and detail that they often complain is lacking in the news coverage. It would also be possible to prepare documentaries on particular problems they wish to address.[11]

Lortie then undercut the promise of this plan with a formula limiting most parties to two four-minute program segments and conceding 60 per cent of all free time to the established parties according to popular vote in the previous election.[12] Despite the timidity of this proposed reapportioning of television, the estab-

---

11   Ibid. p. 406
12   Lortie at this point chooses popular vote as the touchstone for fair allocation. It is a belated admission that he knows the allocation of seats in the House of Commons is unfair and should not be the basis for any other allocation.

lished party leaders and Jim Hawkes' committee on election reform found it too much to contemplate. They decided no change at all would suit them much better.

COURTROOM POLITICS

Preston Manning's Reform Party, denied equitable access to television by the legalized cartel, grabbed a copy of the Lortie report and headed for the Alberta Court of Queen's Bench to test the election broadcast rules against the Charter of Rights and Freedoms. In an astute manoeuvre Reform's lawyers called two of Lortie's principal researchers, Fred Fletcher of York University and Bill Stanbury of the University of British Columbia, as witnesses.

Fletcher, an expert on media and politics, testified that while it is possible to establish a party and run candidates without major television exposure, "to compete effectively and to have a voice in the public debate at the national level requires significant television exposure."[13] Stanbury, an expert on party finances, testified that the retrospective formula for allocating paid political time discriminates against any party which has raised money since the last election. Furthermore "the free time allocations are fundamentally based on the paid time allocations, so if you are up against the wall so to speak on paid time you get proportionally the same amount in free time which reinforces the problem...of unfairness to new, emerging, rapidly growing parties." The court found in favor of the Reform Party and struck down the provisions of the Canada Elections Act regulating the allocation of paid political time, declaring that their discriminatory effects against contender parties outside the House of Commons were excessive and unjustified. It said Parliament can regulate television, but must find a formula more respectful of the charter rights of all parties to freedom of expression and of the voters to an informed vote. A fair formula, the judge suggested in November 1992, could be based

---

13 Reform Party of Canada and Diane Ablonczy vs Attorney General of Canada, Court of Queen's Bench of Alberta, Nov. 30 1992

on the number of candidates nominated by a party before the beginning of the campaign advertising period. Rather than follow that advice, the Mulroney government went to the Alberta Court of Appeal and in June this year got a stay of the lower court's order. The broadcast arbitrator used his discretion earlier this year to dole out a few more minutes to alternative parties but the cartel's television time allocation scheme, despite the savaging administered by both Lortie and the Alberta court, is still the effective law of Canada for the 1993 election.

Other Charter Violations. Reform was by no means the first party to notice that the Canada Elections Act violates the Charter of Rights and it won't be the last. Mel Hurtig's National Party, with a substantial election warchest, a very small time allocation and no place in the leaders' debates, can be expected to attempt an urgent court challenge to the television gag laws before this fall's election advertising period begins. Last year two Quebec New Democrats, Monique Barrette and Daniel Payette, persuaded a Quebec Superior Court judge to rule unconstitutional the anti-small-party landmine which requires a candidate to get 15 per cent of the popular vote to qualify for public subsidies. Again, although Lortie and a court have said the anti-alternative party device cannot survive, the Mulroney government did not amend the law. It stalled by appealing the Quebec decision.

The legal adventures of Reform and the Quebec NDP are child's play compared with the long odyssey of the Green Party through foggy thickets of broadcast regulation and election law in search of the Charter of Rights. The Green Party's chief strategist in these matters for most of the past decade has been Greg Vezina, this book's co-author.

Vezina first tackled the three-party cartel after a 1984 Ontario provincial by-election in an Ottawa-area riding where, as a Green Party candidate, he was excluded from a candidates debate by CJOH, the local CTV affiliate. Vezina persuaded his Liberal opponent, prominent radio announcer Lowell Green, and the Conservative candidate, then-alderman Graham Bird, to withdraw from the debate in protest. CJOH responded by transforming the debate into a solo chat between news director Max Keeping and NDP candidate Evelyn Gigantes who went on to win the election. Vezina filed a complaint to the Canadian Radio-television and Telecommunications Commission (CRTC). During the 1985 Ontario general election the Ottawa CBC affiliate, CBOT, continued to run selective debates among candidates. The big issue in the election was the extension of separate school funding, a policy which had been agreed to by all parties at Queen's Park. The only candidate in the entire region who opposed further separate school funding, Vezina of the Green Party, was excluded from the CBOT debate on the subject. Again he complained to the CRTC which, two years later, issued a caution and a reminder to all broadcasters of their obligations.

In the 1988 federal election the CBC, CTV and Global networks rejected attempts by Seymour Trieger, national leader of the Green Party, to join Mulroney, Turner and Broadbent on the televised leaders debate and provided no alternative platform for the Greens or any of the other smaller parties. On Vezina's advice Trieger complained to the CRTC which, after the election was over, asked the Mulroney government to prosecute the networks for their violation of the Broadcasting Act's television regulations. The government refused to prosecute at which point Vezina and the Green Party undertook to prosecute privately. The CRTC intervened in the action to support its regulation.

Five years and two unfavorable rulings later the matter remains unresolved.[14] The Green Party, represented by former Ontario Attorney General Ian Scott, was to argue again before the Ontario Court of Appeal on October 4 — a date likely to precede some national televised leaders' debates. The Green Party expected to be formally supported by the National Party and other smaller parties in that appearance, in which event any ruling the court made was likely to be appealed to the Supreme Court of Canada. Another action, based on the exclusion of the Greens from the 1990 leaders'

---

14   R. vs. CBC, CTV and Global, Ontario Provincial Division, Kerr, J., March 27, 1991, and Her Majesty the Queen ex. rel. Gregory Vezina vs. CBC, Ontario Court General Division, Borins, J., May 12, 1992.

debate in the Ontario election (where their presence might have turned Bob Rae's NDP majority government into a minority) is also on its way to the Ontario Court of Appeal.

The Green Party prosecution follows the reasoning of Quebec's director-general of elections, Pierre Cote, who ruled that a proposed television debate between Robert Bourassa and then-Premier Pierre-Marc Johnson in 1985 would be, if it excluded leaders of other parties, illegal and potentially could result in the disqualification of all Liberal and Parti Québécois candidates in that election. Cote said a debate involving only the two major party leaders would not be protected by Quebec's free-time broadcast election laws and thus became a valuable political contribution to the chosen parties by the television broadcasters. That, he warned, would attract the sections of the law dealing with corrupt election practices "with all the disastrous consequences this would entail for successful candidates."[15] There were at least two potential violations because Quebec's law contains election expense limits and bans political contributions by corporations. The result, because Bourassa refused a four-leader debate, was no debate in Quebec in 1985 and a subsequent relaxation of the election law.

The Greens, using Cote's logic, are trying to win a place in the national debates by invoking Canada's limits on total election expenses and in Ontario by alleging illegality in the size of the political contribution the broadcasters make to the parties.

The CRTC has confirmed that the networks breached the Broadcasting Act by putting only David Peterson, Bob Rae and Mike Harris on television in 1990 but took no remedial or punitive action. Vezina and the Association of Alternative Political Parties asked the Ontario Elections Commission to prosecute the networks and parties for illegal activity, but it refused. The Ontario commission, composed of Liberals, Conservatives and New

---

15   Cited in Bernier, R. and Monière, D. The Organization of Televised Leaders' Debates in the United States, Europe, Australia and Canada, RC Research, Vol. 18, p. 193

Democrats, also refused Vezina permission to conduct a private prosecution. He asked the Ontario Court of Justice to order the elections commission to authorize prosecution, but there ran afoul of Justice Stephen Borins who dismissed the action with costs against Vezina. No date has been set for the next round at the Ontario Court of Appeal.

The Green Party's frustrating tour of the nether regions of justice has not been entirely futile. In 1991, for example, the television networks planned to exclude both the Greens and the Liberal Party from the British Columbia leaders debate between Rita Johnson and Mike Harcourt. Gordon Wilson's Liberals found their way to the Toronto law firm of Gowling, Strathy and Henderson where Ian Scott and others had been honing their knowledge of broadcast and election law on Vezina's cases. With their help Wilson threatened the networks with legal action and forced his way into the B.C. television debate. With a superior performance he rocketed his previously moribund party overnight from 7 per cent to 37 per cent popular support — and from the fringes of public awareness to official opposition status. The whole B.C. sequence provides proof of the huge and arbitrary implications of television gerrymandering — and of the importance for democracy of ending it. The television networks have since had the pleasure of cutting the amorous Wilson down several notches, but we are left wondering on a different point. In the next televised B.C. leaders' debate will grateful B.C. Liberals insist that a Green share the platform ?

FAIR RULES FOR TELEPOLITICS

The Liberal-Conservative-NDP manipulations of election law may be unravelling under court scrutiny but judges are seldom eager or quick to confront Parliament squarely. The democratization of election broadcasting implied by Reform-Green legal tactics will come about far more quickly and reliably if it is on the agenda of an active popular reform movement.

The changes in broadcast rules proposed here will dovetail neatly with a proportional representation voting system. The present voting system is so unfair to small parties and their supporters, however, that should Canada keep it our modest proposals for equitable treatment of parties on television will be insufficient to level the playing field.

Free time. We endorse the Lortie concept of half-hour magazine-style programs in prime time to allow political parties to present their ideas on their own terms. Within this forum all registered parties should contend in the Danish and Norwegian style — as equals — on condition that they present a full national slate of candidates. Parties running a partial slate would receive a proportionately reduced allocation of television time.

This shift toward party parity in free time allocation is a small but necessary beginning to break the spiral of silence which now afflicts smaller parties in Canadian politics in both news coverage and general discourse — the pervasive assumption, accentuated by British voting rules, that parties which can't win a general election are irrelevant and not worth reporting or talking about.

The fact is that small parties can be consequential even under British voting rules. They sometimes serve as a source of ideas for the larger parties, and sometimes they affect election outcomes. This was apparent in Ontario's 1990 election when the alternative party vote rose, apparently at the expense of the Liberals and Conservatives, and allowed Bob Rae's New Democrats a sneak majority government. It is probably the very sensitivity of the British voting system to small shifts in popular vote which has made the established parties so ruthless in their attempts to exterminate the smaller formations and so cynical in their manipulation of television law. As a royal commission researcher put it:

> The media's continued denigration or exclusion of certain political options tends to discourage individuals from publicly expressing or even privately supporting such options. What is at stake for minor parties is not political power but their very existence as meaningful political players.[16]

---

16   Hackett, Robert. Smaller Voices, RC Research, Vol. 22, p. 190

As Keith Spicer's CRTC phrased it in the 1987 advisory inspired by Vezina's complaints, a broadcaster should not "enjoy the position of a benevolent censor who is able to give the public only what it 'should' know. Nor is it the broadcaster's role to decide in advance which candidates are 'worthy' of broadcast time."[17] For some unknown reason, however, the CRTC has failed to clarify its regulation and by inaction has allowed the broadcasters to continue their unfair and unconstitutional practices. Instead it should be making sure that broadcasting is diverse, that each voter has a full menu of choices, and that each of us has the opportunity to decide personally whose views are worth hearing and whose are not. As the royal commission found, this choice is what the Canadian majority wants. Its surveys showed that 54 per cent of Canadians — far more than are ever likely to vote for alternative parties — think the mass media give too little attention to the ideas and activities of smaller parties. The electorate appears to understand, much better than the parties themselves, that catch-all parties need competitors from which to steal ideas, if only to keep up the pretense of being alive. As Lortie observed:

> The media have been slow to adapt to the increase in the number of registered political parties since 1974 and in particular to the increased public interest in what they have to say. The public demand for greater attention to smaller parties, though fuelled by short-term concerns regarding specific issues, is also part of a general process of expanding participation. Many voters wish to hear views not encompassed by the larger parties. Analyses of voter attitudes suggest that a sense of involvement in the electoral process and participation are likely to be enhanced by a greater diversity of communication channels and perspectives.[18]

With that in mind, we suggest that the allocation of 240 minutes of program time — distributed equally among full-slate national parties and proportionally to all other registered parties — is in-

---

17   Cited in Lortie et al., RC Vol. 1, p. 389
18   Ibid.

complete redress for the wrongs which have been inflicted on smaller parties and the public. In addition, to allow all parties a sustained public presence, a fully national party should be entitled to 28 minutes of free commercial time during the election advertising period, the equivalent of two 30-second spots daily, during prime time or other favorable viewing hours. Again, parties with partial slates would be alloted a fraction of a full share in proportion to candidacies.

In this proposed public service broadcast regime the free time allocation turns entirely on the definition of a registered party and the number of candidates nominated. A registered party for these purposes, we suggest, should be any party running candidates in 15 per cent or more of the constituencies, while a fully national party is one which runs candidates in all the constituencies. A party should also be able to register between elections by presenting, as in Denmark, signatures corresponding to the number of votes cast for each seat in the House of Commons. Based on 1/295 of the 1988 vote, the number of signatures required is 44,000.

Under these arrangements an arbitrator would assign broadcast time to registered parties provisionally according to their campaign plans and finalize the allocation at the close of nominations, which would occur before the campaign advertising period began. Parties failing to nominate candidates in 15 per cent of the ridings would be deregistered.[19] The standard for nominating a constituency candidate should be 300 signatures from residents of the constituency and a bond of $1,000 refundable upon compliance with election expenditure reporting requirements.

Paid political time. The pursuit of funds to pay for commercial television time has been a menace to the solvency of political par-

---

19 The current standard for registered party status is to contest at least 50 constituencies, about 17% of the House of Commons. In the German-style proportional representation system we recommended in Chapter Three there would be 150 constituency MPs, 15 per cent of which would put our proposed standard for party registration at 23 constituency nominations.

ties and a goad to improper fundraising methods in every country where paid advertising is allowed. Still, it may not be desireable or possible under Canada's Charter of Rights to ban paid political television commercials during campaigns. At a cost of $100,000 a minute for full national exposure they are likely to remain the exclusive domain of the larger political parties. We share the view of Bill Stanbury, the Lortie commission's expert on party financing, that there is no need for a separate limitation on televised political advertising. The political parties operate within an overall campaign expenditure limit and it is for them to decide whether scarce funds are best spent on national, regional or local television, radio, newspapers, direct mail, telemarketing or any other form of campaign communication. We would require a broadcaster who sells time to any party to make the same amount available to every other party at the same price.

News and Public Affairs Coverage. Despite the steady increase in political advertising budgets, television news and public affairs coverage remains the most important way in which political parties influence voters.[20] It is likely to remain so even with an improved free time allocation. The TV networks' ritual daily coverage of election tours by major party leaders, and the allotment of news minutes in proportions suspiciously similar to the current formula for paid political time, are well-established practices of the television news business. Long-time NDP strategist Gerry Caplan describes the calculated daily photo opportunities and the planned phrases that an established party leader utters each day as "Gainesburgers" — the morsels political handlers throw to the media pack to keep it from turning savage. Of the election tour experience he says:

---

20   Ibid. p. 376

Nothing is less rational than the process by which the politicians and their flaks have to interact 12 or 15 hours a day with the media that is supposed to be objective and detached about them. It's a remarkable, unique process that is hard to describe and hard to tolerate. I myself hate it.... I hate having to pretend to the media all day long that I think they're terrific and that I have to suck up to them so they put my story on at night.[21]

It is the predictability of these routines of television election coverage, all focused on the major party leaders, which makes the creation of a counterbalancing free time regime so necessary. The alternative, in the name of balanced discourse, is to apply stop-watch-style regulation to the television news operations as is done in some European countries including the United Kingdom. This is a path on which we think most Canadians would prefer not to embark if it can be avoided. We anticipate that, following a switch to proportional representation elections, the television news operations will adjust their methods to the new political realities. In Germany, for example, the small Free Democratic Party is frequently considered newsworthy because of its pivotal role in deciding whether the Social Democrats or Christian Democrats will form the government and the role of its leaders within the governing coalition.

In any event the automatic television news coverage of major party leaders during elections is changing in other ways that require a public policy response. Television news departments are caught between an obligation to provide education in public affairs and a practical need to ensure ratings and commercial survival. The net result has been an industry-wide slide toward "infotainment." In the early days of television, for example, it was not uncommon for election campaign report items to run over two minutes and for the uninterrupted words of party leaders — the "sound bites" — to last much longer than they do today. In the

---

21   Caplan testified at the first trial of the CBC, CTV and Global television networks.

1968 U.S. presidential campaign the average sound bite was 42.3 seconds. By 1988 it had shrunk to 9.8 seconds - barely enough time to intone "I love America, God knows I do, always have and always will." In Canada the phenomenon is not yet so extreme. CBC's The National increased the average length of its leader clips over the course of the 1988 campaign from about 13 seconds at the beginning to nearly 30 seconds apiece during the final week. But here too even the successful politician's direct access to the voter is severely eroded, making free-time broadcasts and other types of broadcasts necessary and important.

Leadership debates. The Lortie commission recognized that leadership debates are a vital element in a democratic election but said they should be left to evolve under the exclusive control of the television networks and established political parties. Lortie may have been prepared to accept, in his own words, "the substantial risk that no debate will be held in any particular campaign or that emerging parties will feel themselves excluded"[22] but this is simply wrongheaded. We, unconstrained by the need to please a prime minister, propose that a party's right to public subsidies be conditional upon its participation in leadership debates.

Debates always have the potential to switch voting intentions and sometimes do. Two thirds of Canadian voters watched some portion of leadership debates during the past two federal elections, and there is evidence that the 1984 confrontation between Brian Mulroney and John Turner switched some Grit support to the Tories, and that Turner's strong attack on free trade in 1988 attracted some votes that would otherwise have gone to the NDP.[23] But the significance of debates is deeper than their impact on the immediate fortunes of any party. They confirm many voters in their intentions. They create more favorable impressions of all the politicians than the public gets from watching news coverage. And

---

22   RC Vol. 1, p. 416
23   Barr, Cathy Widdis. The Importance of Leaders' Debates, RC Research Vol. 18, p. 121

they deepen the electorate's understanding of the political process. Indeed, 78 per cent of Canadians polled by the royal commission wanted more leaders debates, 57 per cent said they should be compulsory, 50 per cent said the leaders of all registered parties should participate and a further 20 per cent said the leaders of all parties in Parliament should participate. We find it revealing that, despite these strong signals from the public, the royal commission couldn't bring itself to the obvious conclusion. It ignored not only the voters but also the clear advice of professor Cathy Widdis Barr of Wilfrid Laurier University, the author of its major research paper on leadership debates. She said debates are public service broadcasts, not news events, and the objections to regulating them don't hold water.

> Debates are an especially significant source of political information among those members of the electorate who have few other information sources. Given this fact, it seems clear that televised leaders debates play a crucial role in our electoral process.... As to whether they should be mandatory, I would have to agree with those who support such a move....Televised debates are the only opportunity — except for party ads and 30-second news bites — that most voters have to see and hear the party leaders.... No individual should have the right to obstruct this process by scuttling a televised debate. This is particularly true given that the individual most likely to refuse to debate is the one who already has the most control over the electoral process — the prime minister.... The evidence presented in this study on the positive impact of debates on the Canadian electorate is sufficient to warrant the institutionalization of debates. Such a move might well infringe on the rights of the media and the political parties. However, whenever the interests of the media, the parties and the voters conflict, the interests of the voters should prevail.[24]

Instead of allowing first ministers to refuse to debate, as did Pierre Trudeau in 1974 and 1979 and Ontario's Frank Miller and

---

24   Ibid. p. 145

Quebec's Robert Bourassa in 1985, the law should provide a broad outline and leave detailed disputes over format, speaking order and the like to be settled by an election official such as the broadcast arbitrator. We suggest two two-hour debates on all networks, one near the beginning of a campaign and another a week before election day. The leaders of all registered parties should participate as formal equals just as candidates for leadership in major political parties are treated as formal equals during party leadership races.

Advocacy Advertising. For all its failed efforts to beautify Canada's three-party political cartel, the Lortie commission from the beginning had only one urgent priority: it wanted to stop non-party political advertising during election campaigns. Parliament had attempted to do just that in 1983, but was thwarted when the National Citizen's Coalition challenged the amendments to the Canada Elections Act. An Alberta court found them to be an unconstitutional infringment of freedom of speech.

The result was that the 1984 and 1988 elections were fought with the political parties operating under spending limits while non-party advocacy groups were free to spend as much as they could muster. By 1988 several interest groups were actively into parallel campaigns. The Campaign Life Coalition, the political wing of the anti-abortion movement, relying mainly on pamphlets and canvassing, targeted candidates in more than 30 ridings who were perceived to be pro-choice while the Coalition for the Protection of Human Life distributed a magazine, *Vitality*, in which it identified 125 candidates from all three established parties who favored the Campaign Life position. The Saskatchewan Pro-Life Association spent $40,000 on a province-wide advertising campaign. Others who got into the act were the Friends of Portage Program for Drug Dependence who spent $45,000 in Montreal and Toronto newspapers calling for more political attention to problems of drug abuse, and the Canadian Peace Pledge Campaign which spent $28,000 denouncing the government and seeking votes for peace candidates.

There was nothing to compare, however, with the mutually reinforcing free trade ad blitzes of the Conservative Party and the Alliance for Free Trade and Job Opportunities, described by Don Murphy of Vickers and Benson Advertising as "the largest, most concentrated promotion campaign ever seen in Canada." *This Magazine* lamented the phenomenon in a cover story titled: "The Big Oink: How Business Swallowed Politics," and Canada elections commissioner George Allen argued publicly that either non-party spending had to be controlled or the Election Act spending limits on parties would have to be abandoned.[25] The Lortie commission agreed that the National Citizens Coalition decision, and Parliament's failure to appeal or repair the damage, created a crisis:

These decisions destroyed the overall effectiveness of the legislative framework for promoting fairness in the exercise of freedom of expression and of democratic rights during Canadian elections. The experience of the 1988 general election clearly demonstrates this. The gaping hole in our existing framework in relation to independent expenditures is patently unfair, and the conundrum that this development presents for electoral reform is now widely acknowledged. Without fairness we may continue to have a "free" society, but we would certainly diminish the democratic character of our society.... It is essential that both Parliament and the courts acknowledge this fundamental fact.....Given the centrality of fairness as a fundamental condition of equality of opportunity in the electoral process, the electoral regulatory framework must be rebuilt. This requires a [Canada Elections Act] with provisions that promote fairness by limiting the election expenses of candidates and parties, by securing access to the broadcast media, and by also limiting, but not ruling out, the opportunity for other individuals and groups to spend independently of candidates and parties during the election period in ways that may directly or indirectly affect the election outcome for at least one candidate or party.[26]

---

25 Kline, Stephen et al., Political Broadcast Advertising in Canada, RC Research, Vol 21, p. 256

26 RC Vol. 1, p. 328

Most Canadians would support that general statement although, as we have tried to make clear, there are far more effective ways to promote electoral fairness than the ones Lortie chose. After stating the problem posed by independent advertising he went on to recommend a spending limit of $1,000 for every private individual and non-party advocacy group during election campaigns, with no pooling of individual limits. "The effect of this limit would most likely be to restrict the amount of money spent on media advertising," said Lortie, boldly staking out his claim as a comic. The effective ban on non-party advertising was embraced by the Hawkes committee and quickly incorporated into the Canada Elections Act by the House of Commons on a quiet Friday afternoon before Parliament's Easter break this year, along with the various provisions described in Chapter Two designed to eradicate small political parties.

It is difficult to believe that either Lortie or the members of the Hawkes committee expected to fool anyone. David Sommerville and the National Citizen's Coalition were quick to bring the matter to attention of the friendly Alberta Court of Queen's Bench, which again ruled Parliament's labors unconstitutional. Clearly what Canada needs, and what the constitution requires, is a method of restraining independent advocacy during elections, especially on television, without gagging it. The solution lies in the fairness doctrine, long established in both Canadian and U.S. broadcast law, which holds that broadcasters who air controversial issues of public importance must provide reasonable opportunities for the presentation of conflicting viewpoints — a right of reply.[27]

Citizens and groups should be allowed to spend to advocate their political beliefs and interests during campaigns, but only upon meeting some conditions: those spending more than $5,000 should be required to register their intention and later an accounting of the expenditure and list of contributors with the chief electoral officer; the officer should be able to assign them to an

---

27   Graber, Doris. The Mass Media and Election Campaigns in the United States of America, RC Research Vol. 19, p. 122

umbrella group if several groups are promoting similar objectives; and no individual, group or umbrella group should spend more than 15 per cent of the campaign expense limit for a registered national party. Currently that would set an outside limit on private spending on one side of an issue of about $1.5 million, an amount ample for expression but not so large as to overwhelm the political parties.

We propose that broadcasters giving or selling time for non-party advocacy should be required by law to offer, at no charge, a right of reply to any umbrella group which forms in reaction to a private advocacy campaign. The free time for reply should be half the amount of time devoted to the advocacy, and the opposing group should be entitled to buy as much again to equalize the broadcast time of the two campaigns. In this way freedom of expression, freedom of the media and the right of voters to be informed and have a fair election all can be adequately protected.

Polling. Political parties make extensive use of polling to plot their election strategy and advertising campaigns, and the major television networks and newspapers have made reporting of poll results a major feature of their election coverage. Twenty-two polls were reported during the 1988 campaign, double the number reported in 1984. The ubiquitous polling information is one of the factors which diverts journalistic and public attention from party differences on issues to the "horse-race" dimension of the campaign — a fixation on who will win rather than an examination of the alternative consequences. Thirty per cent of all television news election items in 1988 included reference to opinion polls.[28]

The danger of rogue, phantom or inaccurate polls is sufficiently great to warrant an enforceable publication blackout as recommended by the Lortie commission and passed into law this spring. No polls are to be published during the 72 hours prior to the start of balloting. Beyond that more attention is needed to ensure that

---

28   RC Vol. 1, p. 458

such widely reported and closely followed information, which can produce bandwagon effects and which many Canadians take into account in their negative or strategic voting decisions, is as accurate as possible. Until now, despite their scientific aura, all political polls conducted in Canada have suffered from a significant blind spot. A recent Environics polling experiment discovered that standard polling practice badly underrates alternative political parties. Using its standard questioning technique, which identifies the three established parties and Reform or the Bloc Québécois, Environics found only 2 per cent of respondents in March 1993 said they would vote for some other party. Three months later when the surveyors showed respondents a card naming 13 registered political parties, support for parties other than the five usually named leaped to 10 per cent — a startling five-fold increase. This confirms what small-party activists have always known: their support on election day, when party names are shown on the ballot, is several times greater than it appears to be in surveys which neglect to name them and rely on the dismissive category "Other." The phenomenon was apparent during the 1990 Ontario election, when pre-election polling put the alternative parties at 2 per cent and their final tally was a surprising 7 per cent of the total.

In the interests of informed voting we support the Lortie recommendation that any news organization that sponsors, buys or acquires an opinion poll and is the first to announce its results during an election campaign be required by law to include information on the poll's methodology including: the name of the polling organization; the sponsor who paid for it; the dates of the interviewing period; the collection method (telephone, interview, mailed questionnaire); the population from which the sample was drawn; the number of respondents; the refusal rate; the margin of error; the exact wording of the question reported; and the size, description and margin of error for any subsamples used in the

182

report.[29] To that we add that to be reportable an election poll should identify all registered political parties to the respondents, and that the media should be required to report the results for each of those parties. In the same vein the television networks should be required when reporting election results to name and give the vote for each registered political party.

POLITICAL PARTY ACCESS TO THE PUBLIC

Ensuring that we the voters can hear the pitch of all parties during the election period through debates, free time broadcasts and more careful balancing of public affairs programs will broaden and improve Canada's political discourse, but much more is required. Elections by their nature involve the parties in a burst of effort to consolidate and identify their supporters and get them to the voting booths. Voter education is a very different continuous process and the broadcasting regime in particular should acknowledge that fact.

Prime Time Political Broadcasts. We should be allowed unfiltered, unmediated access to the messages of all registered political parties on a regular basis. The most obvious method to achieve this is to require broadcasters, by law, to provide ongoing free time to political parties. We propose a prime time 30-minute weekly magazine program in the same style as the election period broadcast with time allocated among the parties using the free-time election formula updated at regular intervals.

Interviews, Actualities, and Fireside Chats. The television networks and their news departments guard their editorial independence and freedom jealously, but there is a great deal of broadcast activity which is not news and which is clearly partisan in nature. A New Year's fireside chat with the Prime Minister, although the networks may hope news will result, is not news. Hour upon hour of Conservative, Liberal or NDP leadership convention

---

29   Ibid. p. 464

coverage, while it may hold some interest for political junkies, is not news. Both types of event are, in effect, extended free promotions of the politicians and parties involved. In the name of fairness and balance the broadcasters should be required, by law, to provide compensating exposure to other registered political parties. For example, the panels of spin doctors and major party MPs used to provide commentary during the lengthy breaks at conventions could easily be supplemented by panels of alternative party representatives.

Cable Television. The greatest opportunity to liberate Canada's political discourse from the straightjacket of the television news formula and the 15 second sound bite is offered by cable television, which reaches more than 70 per cent of all Canadian households. The cable's potential for democratic broadcasting is at present seriously underdeveloped although cable companies and community cable programming cooperatives are, generally speaking, far more egalitarian in their programming impulses than either Parliament or the television networks. Election debates on cable, for example, often involve candidates from all registered parties on an equal time basis. But the cable companies are unlikely to invest more heavily than they now do in extensive programming efforts.

CBC Newsworld, the public corporation's all-news specialty cable channel, said when it sought licensing from the CRTC that it would present more coverage of alternative political parties than was available on the main CBC network. It promised "a greater variety of news sources from interested communities, including social movements, multicultural groups, and political parties" and a forum for "distant and different voices from all parts of Canada" during and between elections. It hasn't happened, and the Lortie commission research explains why.

> As a second window on the regular network, the news channel will be relying on news programming, both national and local, in which the constraints of time and conventional journalistic notions of balance are in full force. These factors, which have traditionally excluded minority parties and interests from being fully represented

on the regular channels of the Canadian broadcasting system, will continue to govern much of Newsworld's programming at source.... Most importantly, the Newsworld organization does not recognize any special obligation to provide public access under its current charter.... Trina McQueen said that Newsworld will act like any other broadcaster to ensure that its coverage is fair and balanced in a federal election.... We believe that the equation of more news with more diverse news is inherently problematic in Canada.... Newsworld seems to have been developed and conceived as a service offering Canadians more of the same — familiar news sources and news perspectives — in a new cable package.[30]

The Canadian Parliamentary Channel, a consortium of the CBC, some cable operators and the House of Commons, applied in 1989 for a CRTC licence to expand from its electronic Hansard role to cover "national political party activities, public discussion and participation, provincial affairs, and other public events of national significance." Since then, however, the cash-strapped CBC has backed out of its $3.7 million yearly financial commitment to the channel and it has been operating unlicenced. Lortie recommended that the channel carry repeats of free-time political broadcasts, but the idea of broadcasting any political messages other than those provided by the elected politicians in the House of Commons and its committees does not find favor on the Hill. "To ensure a high level of objectivity and integrity of our programming we have abstained from doing any partisan programming," said general manager Martha Wilson in a recent letter explaining why the channel refuses material from registered parties outside the House of Commons.[31] She has, understandably, adopted the semantics of the cartel which employs her: pumping out three sets of partisan messages from Parliament is deemed non-partisan activity.

---

30 Hogarth, David and Gilsdorf, William. The Impact of All-News Services on Election and Election Coverage, RC Research Vol. 21, p. 164
31 Letter to Jim Harris of the Association of Political Parties Committed to Democracy, July 5, 1993

From all this it seems there are no significant prospects for change in the current diet of political programming on television in the absence of the political shakeup we propose in the next chapter. We see two ways in which television offerings might be diversified, but both require an exercise of will which has not been in evidence. Keith Spicer and his CRTC colleagues could get tough with Newsworld and the Canadian Parliamentary Channel and demand that they provide or open themselves to more varied political programming in the widest interpretation of the Broadcasting Act. The probability of that happening, and of those organizations taking up the challenge with any flair, is close to zero. Another option, and in our opinion the only one with real potential, is for the CRTC to licence a specialty channel explicitly devoted to the expression of diverse minority views and make it part of the basic cable service.[32]

Our conclusion, after this tour of the electronic domain, is that the only apparent force for change in the political balance of Canadian television is the Charter of Rights. The court cases, however, are by their nature slow, expensive and uncertain in outcome. Real democrats will want to find another way to promote change, and to that challenge we now turn.

---

32 One of the authors, Greg Vezina, is co-founder of The Democracy Channel Inc., a corporation which plans to apply to the CRTC to be licensed as a specialty public access channel on basic cable. Its proposal to investors describes the need for "responsible — and responsive — public interest television" and states that the channel will put political reform on the public agenda, provide equal opportunity exposure for all registered political parties, give a soap-box to "inventors, social planners, activists — people with ideas," and encourage broad public participation through video mail and national open line programs.

7

TAKING CONTROL:
THE DEMOCRACY LEAGUE

WE WANT A DEMOCRACY that works better and the major elements of a democratic reform agenda are known to us. Before all else we need the citizen Initiative as our democratic sword — a permanent reminder to Members of Parliament and all the other powers-that-be that the people are sovereign and that, if necessary, we can propose, amend or reject any law. With the Initiative we will bury once and for all the Mulroney Doctrine — the pernicious proposition that a government with a majority in Parliament can do whatever it wants.

Then we need proportional representation elections to make every vote count equally, to make Parliament a more faithful reflection of the diverse currents in Canadian society, and to make political parties more loyal and more accountable to their members and voters. These two major reforms, aided by further initiatives as required, will carry us toward the open government and open communications system which should be the goal and pride of a free people.

The difficulty is that our established political parties want none of this. They titillate with insincere hints at reform but they are incapable of serious or sustained self-criticism. Instead they are devout, dedicated and devious in defence of a failed status quo. We the voters, if we are to refashion Canadian democracy, will need a plan which does not depend on the good will or good faith of the established parties. We will have to create an organization

— a Democracy League — to act as an information centre assisting hundreds of self-selected citizen groups which will, each in their own way, act to bring about the changes Canadians want and need. The Democracy League, unlike the Progressive Party and other populist reform movements since, will not be a political party. It will be nowhere and everywhere on the ideological dial because it will have no general program for governing Canadian society. The sole objective will be to reform the democratic process itself and in this Canadians of every political persuasion, to their own amazement and satisfaction, will cooperate. The Democracy League will die a natural death when its limited goals are achieved and the new rules of democratic competition for political power are in place.

THE 1993 ELECTION

The immediate democratic question for Canadians in the fall of 1993 is, naturally enough, how to mark our ballots in the federal election. Democratic reform is not high on the official political agenda at the moment and its future will not be directly addressed one way or another by the upcoming vote. For the Progressive Conservatives, Liberals and New Democrats, democratic reform is no issue at all or one which, with a small effort, can be postponed indefinitely. There are, however, three alternative parties which have made democratic reform prominent in their election platforms and which for that reason deserve attention from voters who want to use the ballot to signal that reform is their top priority.

The Green Party of Canada, in addition to its emphasis on environmental protection, has for a decade advocated proportional representation — the voting system which made possible the party's notable political breakthrough in Germany and the election of Green representatives in several other countries. The Greens do not have an official position on the Initiative, but as an organization suspicious of hierarchy and built on democratic participation the party can be expected to be friendly to the proposal. The National Party of Canada led by Mel Hurtig has put democratic reform at the heart of its program with clear commitments to proportional representation elections, pay-per-vote public financing of political parties, and referendums on major government policies. Although the Initiative is not official party policy, it would be a very short reach for the National Party to support it.

Some supporters of democratic reform will be uncomfortable with any vote that appears to endorse the perceived leftist tilt of the Greens or the economic nationalism and state interventionism of the National Party. These voters should consider Preston Manning's Reform Party, whose program explicitly endorses the statutory Initiative based on petitions from 3 per cent of the voting electorate. The Reform Party of Canada is at the moment the largest formation in the field which has made direct democracy part of its essential political identity and commitment, and its clear position already has forced Prime Minister Kim Campbell to pretend interest in the Initiative.

We note again that both large outsider parties in this election, Reform and the Bloc Québécois, have shown no speck of interest in proportional representation voting. Both, we suggest, are still suffering from the ideological disease which afflicts many political minorities in Canada — an urge to profit from the unfair electoral system, achieve unwarranted control over Parliament, and use the state to impose a minority social and political vision on the rest of the population. The polling information presented in Chapter One indicates, unless there are drastic shifts in public opinion during the campaign, that the Bloc Québécois will indeed succeed in winning seats far beyond the measure of its popular support in Quebec. In the West by contrast the Reform Party appears not to be over the hump and is likely to win many fewer seats than its voting support warrants. If we are right, Reform faces a simple choice: to roll up and die like many previous protest movements, or to reposition itself in a broader campaign for democratic reform including proportional representation. We think the second choice makes more sense for Reform and, because the party represents a significant segment of public opinion which deserves principled representation in Parliament, more sense for Canada.

In Quebec the program of the Democracy League is likely to prove attractive to Forum Option-Jeunesse, the new youth movement led by former Liberal youth president Mario Dumont and to its ally Group Reflexion-Quebec, Jean Allaire's gathering of intellectuals and businessmen, all of whom are trying to articulate a political alternative to the political standoff between the federalist Liberal party and the separatist Parti Québécois. Talk of a third party in Quebec is in the air[1] and there can be nothing more central to such an undertaking than to make sure that the electoral rules permit its survival and growth.

The Environics polling data suggest that the Progressive Conservatives will do badly in every province and will end up this fall with many fewer seats than their popular vote deserves. The NDP similarly appears to be in dire trouble everywhere except Saskatchewan, where a 36 per cent vote may be enough to win in most seats. At the moment only two parties stand to benefit from the distorted logic of our electoral system — the Bloc Québécois, which wants to break up Canada, and the Liberal Party, which may be on the verge of winning the biggest, phoniest parliamentary majority in Canadian history. The Liberals nationally could be in a position a bit like Bob Rae's New Democrats in Ontario or Brian Mulroney's Conservatives after 1988, governing with a technical majority but lacking the legitimacy that a popular majority provides. Even some Liberals may concede that the outcome is not healthy or reasonable.

Indeed, when the dust settles after the fall vote, some New Democrats concerned for the survival of their federal party and some Progressive Conservatives distressed at the prospect of another generation in the electoral wilderness may finally admit that proportional representation is, in fact, an excellent idea. Some Liberals — the few able to see over the rim of the Ottawa pork barrel — will also realize that the political system needs reform and that the established party which first moves to embrace it will earn — and deserve — substantial public gratitude.

---

1   Mackenzie, Robert. Allaire May Build New Party, *Toronto Star*, July 19, 1993

THE DEMOCRACY LEAGUE

The challenge for real democrats, once the federal election is over, will be to encourage and accelerate the embryonic reform impulse within each of the established political parties until their consensus against change has become a consensus for reform. There are two possible political styles for pursuing the project, supplication and high-pressure tactics. We propose that the Democracy League use both, but with the main emphasis on political hardball. The currency of electoral politics is seats in legislatures and the Democracy League should set about, within all three established political parties, to target and unseat every elected representative who refuses to endorse and speak publicly in favor of the democratic reform program. It should at the same time begin the much easier task, as the nominations come up, of taking over every party riding association where there is no sitting member.

Because the nomination of candidates is the only point at which decisive pressure can be brought to bear on all the political parties, and because the next federal Parliament is likely to last four years, there will probably be little opportunity to carry out this democratic mission at the federal level in the next two or three years. For that reason the initial campaigns of the Democracy League will in all probability focus on the members of the established parties in provincial legislatures as they come up for re-election. Since the provincial legislatures often display distortions in representation even worse than those in the federal Parliament this is a task which must be undertaken at some point anyway, and it will provide Democracy League activists with good practice for taking over the federal political parties in 1996 and 1997.

The strategy is simple and, given a reasonable commitment by real democrats, it cannot fail. The first riding association challenges will rivet the attention of the political elites and put the Democracy League program on the public agenda. Each unseating of an incumbent MP, MPP or MLA will spread news of the Democracy League and encourage other democrats all across Canada to increase their own efforts. We anticipate that first one and then all three of the established political parties will decide, rather than play the scenario out to its conclusion, to surrender and embrace the program of the Democracy League. The questions of Initiative and electoral reform will be put to the Canadian people by referendum for a democratic verdict, and we will vote for reform. If the parties are slow to reach the necessary decisions, Democracy League activists will continue to pile up control over more and more riding associations. The showdowns will then take place at party policy conferences or leadership conventions where Liberals for Democracy, Progressive Conservatives for Democracy, or New Democrats for Democracy will be in the majority and will turn the top party officials out to pasture. Our bet is that the party establishments will see the light long before their personal positions are so directly in jeopardy. If they do not the Democracy League, by controlling nominations in all parties, will in theory end up holding a majority in Parliament. In that very unlikely event it will legislate the Initiative and proportional representation and dissolve Parliament for new elections under the new rules.

All this can be accomplished quite easily provided that real democrats remember the only essential rule of party infighting: the majority rules. In the final analysis Democracy League activists will have to recruit a sufficient number of new party members to be able to outvote opponents within each riding association. To do that efficiently it will be helpful to be aware of the opponent's plans so the early standardbearers of the League will take out memberships in party riding associations, campus or women's associations, volunteer for activity assisting the executive, and then run for a position on the executive. Seeking an executive position, which is generally easy to come by, confers a right to the list of party members as well as information about executive meeting schedules and the like. Such intelligence will assist the organization and effectiveness of the Democracy League chapter in each electoral constituency.

Bringing about political change by encouraging groups to get involved in the political parties is, of course, not a new idea. In fact, it seems to be the sort of thing Prime Minister Kim Campbell was inviting when, while seeking the Conservative leadership, she said:

> I don't believe that democratic institutions run on autopilot. The thing that infuriates me is apathy — people who boast about how they've never been involved in a political party. Who do they think is working to keep this society intact so they can have the luxury of sitting back and being such condescending SOBs? To hell with them.[2]

Political parties, with their tiny elites and their small, inactive memberships are like empty vessels waiting for someone to come along, fill them up and make use of them. The use may be personal — Brian Mulroney's lengthy ego trip in pursuit of the Conservative leadership comes to mind — or ideological. Nearly 25 years ago the left-wing and nationalist Waffle movement in the NDP led by James Laxer made a strong bid to capture the party leadership and came surprisingly close to pulling it off. In the United States the organised invasion of the Republican Party by religious fundamentalists at the urging of TV evangelists Jerry Falwell and Pat Robertson, and their important role in propelling Ronald Reagan to the presidency are a good illustration of how a party can be transformed by people with a mission. In Canada the "family values" forces have made similar incursions into both the Liberal and Conservative parties. The anti-abortion Liberals for Life, although ultimately unsuccessful in their bid for influence, have caused a considerable stir in the Liberal Party. One of their leaders, Tom Wappel, gained election to Parliament as the MP for Scarborough West and ran for the leadership of the Liberal party in 1990. MP John Nunziata (York South-Weston) another leadership candidate, dismissed the Liberals for Life as a minor phenomenon exaggerated by media attention and labelled Dan McCash, an organiser of the new group, a self-seeking opportunist. Nunziata even alleged that the Liberals for Life asked him for

---

2   Newman, Peter. Citizen Kim, *Vancouver Magazine*, May 1993

$50,000 as the price of its assistance in the struggle for Liberal leadership delegates. Wappel, however, has a different read on what was happening. Although he finished a distant fourth behind Jean Chrétien in the contest to replace John Turner, Wappel said Liberals for Life were and are a significant presence in the Liberal party. They helped him capture the majority of Liberal leadership convention delegates from Saskatchewan and to finish second in more ridings than either Paul Martin or Sheila Copps. In his view the Liberal party's decision to change its constitution, allowing leader Jean Chrétien to set aside riding association nominations and appoint candidates, was due primarily to fear of the growing impact of Liberals for Life. Party officials close to Chrétien confirm that a failed attempt by Liberals for Life to take over the entire executive of the federal Liberal Party at a convention in February 1992 was a "wake-up call" that the party establishment has not ignored. Chrétien, who was trying to increase the number of female candidates running in winnable ridings this year, killed two birds with one stone by appointing women to some ridings where Liberals for Life men were poised to win the nomination — Etobicoke-Lakeshore, Beaches-Woodbine, Simcoe North and Saskatoon-Humboldt. As Wappel sees it, the upper echelons of the Liberal Party remain dominated by pro-choice types who stay in control "because not enough people have joined the party to challenge them."

During this year's Conservative leadership contest there was incessant talk of family values as all the leadership candidates vied for the support of an important block of delegates. In particular the campaign of MP Jim Edwards (Edmonton Southwest) was rooted strongly in Alberta's bible belt, and it was Edwards' move to Campbell which put her over the top and into the Prime Minister's office.

The religious minorities are within their legal rights to organise, concentrate their influence and manipulate the dominant political parties but their activities make the majority, who can't be sure just how much influence they have acquired, justifiably nervous. The vulnerability of the Liberal and Conservative parties to sectarian takeover, or even a co-ordinated double takeover, is a further argument for an electoral system which gives voters a greater array of party choice. Under proportional representation rules, where it is possible to elect representatives from four, five or six significant political parties instead of two, the short term consequences of any party being captured by narrow interests are greatly reduced and the longer term consequences are negligible. Until we change the voting rules, however, the internal vulnerability of the parties is simply a reality waiting to be exploited by any group with the cohesion and determination to do it.

What Canadians have been catching occasional glimpses of during these struggles within the brokerage parties is a type of coalition politics — a secret politics carried out by unrepresentative cabals. When there are deals and accommodations their terms are unknown and become hidden baggage which slips past the electorate under the usual labels — Liberal, Progressive Conservative and New Democrat. Far better, we say, to create an electoral system in which the family values crowd, the Wafflers and economic nationalists and other highly-motivated minority groups find it both possible and necessary to identify themselves as political parties. Their attempts to reshape society will then be clearly visible as inter-party bargaining within the Parliament of Canada and the provincial legislatures, and the people of Canada will be in a position to monitor the political bargains and pass democratic judgment on them.

The two old parties have no monopoly on internal coalitions or on faction-fighting as the Ontario NDP is currently demonstrating with a spectacular display of dissension within an established party. Since its election in 1990 Bob Rae's NDP government has abandoned nearly everything the party stood for during five decades in opposition — public auto insurance, job creation above fiscal restraint, the sanctity of collective bargaining, pension reform, industrial strategy, a better deal for the poor, the primacy of the Environmental Assessment Act, even its opposition to legalized gambling. Rae's most audacious improvisation has been to legislate wage freezes and job cuts to the public service and call it a social contract. The response of the labor leaders who installed Rae as leader has been highly equivocal and nobody personifies

195

their dilemma better than Julie Davis — president of the Ontario NDP, chairperson of its 1990 election campaign, chairperson of the current federal NDP campaign, secretary-treasurer of the Ontario Federation of Labor, and a former negotiator for hospital workers represented by the Canadian Union of Public Employees. "I feel as if someone has reached in and ripped my heart out," said Davis the day the NDP's manufactured majority in the Ontario legislature adopted the cutback law.[3]

More interesting than how the labor leaders feel is the question of what they will now do. A number have said publicly that their financial and manpower commitments to the NDP will be scaled back or eliminated, but such threats at this long remove from the next Ontario election won't cause Rae to lose much sleep. His controversial strategy assumes that the electorate will begin to perceive the Ontario NDP as a genuine party of government which has liberated itself from overdependence on organised labor and has become an open brokerage party like the Liberals and Conservatives. At the same time Rae is assuming that, come the next election, traditional NDP supporters who now feel betrayed will realize they have no place to take their energies or their votes — because the Liberals and Conservatives will treat them even worse.

In this context the public suggestions from Canadian Labor Congress president Bob White and CAW president Buzz Hargrove that labor will pull back a step from the NDP and refocus on extraparliamentary political activity is consistent with Rae's moves to redefine the NDP as a freelance brokerage party rather than a party of political principle or a party acting for an organized labor clientele. Public sector unionists like Davis and Ontario CUPE President Sid Ryan, whose members' welfare depends directly on the fiscal policies of the Ontario government, are not as willing as private sector unionists like White, Hargrove and Steelworker boss

---

3   *Toronto Star,* July 8, 1993

Leo Gerard to allow the political decoupling to proceed uncontested.

Davis, with a foot in all camps, stated the alternative obliquely:

> We (the labor movement) will stay in the party to fight for what we believe are social democratic principles. The party doesn't belong to just the 71 members of the caucus.[4]

Ryan, accountable only to his public sector members, posed the alternative to the Rae-White decoupling strategy nakedly. His union, with 165,000 members in Ontario, will try to unseat the 66 Ontario MPPs who voted for Rae's cutback laws when they seek renomination.

> In the case of these MPPs here today we will find candidates within labor to oppose them in the riding associations for the next election. And those that survive those riding association elections will not receive one little bit of help, financial or otherwise, from labor.[5]

What the CUPE leaders and other public sector labor leaders like Liz Barkley, head of the 46,000-member Ontario Secondary School Teachers Federation, have not yet faced up to is this: within the logic of the present electoral system, the Rae-White decision to reposition the NDP more clearly as a brokerage party makes sense. Rae is simply trying to consolidate the new support he won in 1990 by imitating former Ontario Conservative premier Bill Davis, a politician who for 14 years turned the practice of single-party minority government in three-party Ontario into an art form. It was said that Davis rarely decided what to have for breakfast without consulting opinion polls, and his moderate conservatism punctuated by the occasional theft of popular NDP or Liberal policies — buying an oil company, for example, or stopping an expressway — used to drive true believers on the right

---

4   Ibid.
5   Ibid.

wing of the Conservative party into frenzies of frustration. Rae is now attempting to use the same strategy from the other side of the left-right divide. It is risky, because it is not obvious that Ontario actually needs three brokerage parties or that the NDP base can withstand the psychological shock, but what Rae is attempting is certainly not ridiculous.

All those New Democrats like Ryan and Davis who want the Ontario NDP to remain a labor-oriented social democratic party must accept the corollary: such an NDP will always be at risk of electoral disaster unless Ontario switches to proportional representation voting rules. In that respect the interests of the Ontario NDP as they envisage it now coincide directly with the interests of the federal NDP: both need electoral reform to survive. We invite Davis, Ryan and the many others who share their outlook to form chapters of the Democracy League and put on New Democrats for Democracy buttons as they set out to nuke the 66 wayward Ontario MPPs. Revenge is not an unknown motive in politics, but a positive program is far more interesting and effective.

While trade unionists and federal NDP activists launch Democracy League activity within the controlling provincial sections of the NDP, others will take up the cause as Liberals for Democracy and Progressive Conservatives for Democracy. Some will already be members of those parties, but most will join for the avowed purpose of bringing about democratic change. The campaigns will advance more rapidly if organized groups outside the parties , such as the trade unions, take collective decisions to join the Democracy League and take on a project — the conquest of a party riding association or several of them.

There are many other organizations which, if they consider their political objectives, will realize that the Democracy League's program is right up their alley. Consider, for example, the National Action Committee on the Status of Women, an umbrella group of 500 organizations with a combined strength of two million members. It wants to see more women elected to Parliament on the presumption that women representatives will advance women's interests in such matters as publicly-financed child care. NAC leaders already know that proportional representation electoral systems put more women into legislatures. Anyone who doubts whether that would happen in Canada need only consider the probable effect under PR voting rules if NAC circulated a petition, obtained 44,000 signatures, and registered the Women's Party of Canada for the next general election. Every other political party, out of a simple and primitive desire to hold its female vote, would beg able women to take constituency nominations or accept safe positions on the party list. The gender transformation of the Parliament of Canada, now scheduled to take forever, would occur with astonishing speed. If we are right, tens of thousands of NAC members from the unions, teacher federations, nursing associations, churches, business and professional women's clubs, the student movement, and the birth control, sexual assault and women's shelter centres should be willing and eager to join all three political parties to force through the needed democratic reforms.

Another group which should find the Democracy League attractive is the National Citizen's Coalition. Its participatory advertising campaigns against new taxes, government spending abuses and politicians' perquisites are like training runs for the real political decision-making offered by the citizen Initiative. David Sommerville and other NCC activists are among those Canadians who think that the Mulroney government was not resolute enough in its war on government spending, and their message has won a substantial following. To work as hard as these strict conservatives have for more than a decade, to succeed in shifting public opinion, and then to see an archaic electoral system fabricate a contrary result in Parliament as it will this fall, should be enough to provoke new thinking in neo-conservative circles about the practice of representative democracy.

The environmental movement, which during the recession has lost the political spotlight but lives on in the hearts and minds of hundreds of thousands of Canadians, desperately needs proportional representation. In Germany, where the electoral system does not deem a Green vote to be a wasted vote, that party has commanded as much as 8 per cent popular support. A presence in Parliament, and the financial and leadership resources that go with it, would be a boon for the movement and for Canada. For years insiders from established parties have joined the Green Party to paralyse it by abusing its consensual decision-making procedures. The time has come for the Greens, Greenpeace, Pollution Probe, Friends of the Earth, the Western Canada Wilderness Society and all other committed environmentalists to join the established parties as agents of the Democracy League to show them what Greens can do when playing by standard political rules.

The consumer protection movement — large, diverse, socially useful and weakly organised — needs the Democracy League. In our political system consumer protection concerns are almost always subordinated to the lobby power of producer groups, as Ken Rubin recently reminded us by showing how the Canada Food Guide's health advice was watered down by the egg and meat marketing agencies. The diffuse consumer interest can be made politically effective, not through the political parties, but by the direct democratic action of petition and Initiative. Just as Ralph Nader tried to launch a national Initiative law in the United States, we expect the Consumers Association of Canada and other organised consumer groups to take up the Democracy League project. The difference will be that, due to differences in the two political systems, we Canadians have an easier task and we will succeed.

There are almost certainly other organised interests which would benefit from the Democracy League program and which will decide to take part. One obvious source of activists, aside from Green Party and Reform Party members, will be the members of all the other alternative political parties now oppressed by the devastating combination of British voting rules and television gerrymandering. As the Democracy League juggernaut starts to roll the established parties will complain that it is unethical for some League members to belong to more than one registered political party at a time.

We suspect that Canadians are in no mood to hear lectures on political ethics from the politicians of the established parties. One of us, Greg Vezina, started as a Conservative, resigned to become a Green, and has openly held memberships in the Green Party of Canada and the Ontario Progressive Conservative Party since 1987 without attracting sanctions from either party. The existence of crossover artists —

people who find it expedient to be a provincial Liberal and federal Conservative, or provincial Conservative and federal Liberal — is well-known. Business corporations find it politic and prudent to support the Liberal and Conservative parties simultaneously. There is some evidence, as we noted in Chapter Two, of the Liberals and Conservatives sharing the same members in some ridings while for many years in British Columbia they shared the same provincial party — Social Credit. We saw in Chapter Six how the federal parties colluded and rigged the Canada Elections Act to inhibit challenges to their monopoly. In all these circumstances any real democrat who holds multiple memberships during the upcoming Democracy League campaigns may be offending party rules but cannot be said to be offending any higher principle. In this domain there are at present no higher principles to be found.

Finally, although the speed of the Democracy League's progress will probably depend on the actions of coalitions of organised groups, there is a prior need for a few energetic organisers to get it off the ground and an ongoing need for individual Canadians who want to be part of the action. This book and the petition in Appendix A provide the tools any real democrat needs to fire the opening salvos for the Democracy League in an organization or in their neighborhood. Those who wish to take part in organizing a steering committee and communications system for the Democracy League and help prepare its constitution are invited to contact the authors at this address:

The Democracy League
112 Parliament St.
Toronto, Ontario
M5A 2Y8

Our parting thought after our exploration of the dysfunctional Canadian political system in 1993 is as follows. A citizen must be more than a voter. Democracy is supposed to be government by the people and it is high time we organized ourselves to give it a serious try.

APPENDICES

These materials — petitions, extracts from party constitutions, examples of meeting procedure — are intended to give readers a feel for the terrain on which the Democracy League's campaigns will be conducted. Serious players will, of course, want to acquire the appropriate documents for the parties and riding associations in which they become involved. Our attention in what follows is focused primarily on the Liberal and Progressive Conservative parties because until one of those two dominant parties is obliged to adopt the reform program the electoral laws cannot be changed.

APPENDIX A

PETITION
TO THE HONOURABLE HOUSE OF COMMONS CANADA
IN PARLIAMENT ASSEMBLED

The petition of the undersigned citizens of Canada who now avail themselves of their inalienable right to present a grievance common to your Petitioners in the certain assurance that your honourable House will therefore provide a remedy.

HUMBLY SHEWETH

WHEREAS the voters in Canada want more direct control of their elected representatives in Parliament.

WHEREAS the voters in Canada want more direct control in public policy and governance.

WHEREAS the Royal Commission on Electoral Reform and Party Finance has confirmed public suspicions that there are many inequities in our current election laws.

WHEREAS the Chief Elections Officer reported such problems to Parliament, as duty bound, after the 1984 and 1988 Elections and requested action by Parliament.

WHEREAS several courts have ruled sections of our electoral law unconstitutional, and the Government has asked the courts to suspend such decisions while under appeal so it could continue to conduct elections under unconstitutional rules and practices.

WHEREAS Parliament has chosen not to act to rectify these problems or deal with these exigencies.

WHEREAS the Spicer Citizens' Forum found that Canadians want to be more directly involved in government decisions.

WHEREFORE the undersigned, your petitioners, humbly pray and call upon Parliament to enact legislation to allow 3% of the number of voters who cast ballots in the previous election to initiate, through the petition process, a binding referendum on any issue so petitioned.

AND as in duty bound your Petitioners will ever pray.

DATE _____

PETITION TO:

have Parliament enact legislation to allow 3% of the number of voters who cast ballots in the previous election to initiate, through the petition process, a binding referendum.

SIGNATURE	ADDRESS	POSTAL CODE

1._____

2._____

3._____

4._____

5._____

6._____

7._____

8._____

9._____

10._____

11._____

12._____

13._____

14._____

15._____

16._____

17._____

18._____

19._____

20._____

21._____

22 _____

23._____

24._____

25._____

26._____

27._____

28._____

29._____

30._____

APPENDIX B

PETITION
TO THE HONOURABLE HOUSE OF COMMONS CANADA
IN PARLIAMENT ASSEMBLED

The petition of the undersigned citizens of Canada who now avail themselves of their inalienable right to present a grievance common to your Petitioners in the certain assurance that your honourable House will therefore provide a remedy.

HUMBLY SHEWETH

WHEREAS the voters in Canada want more direct control of their elected representatives in Parliament.

WHEREAS the voters in Canada want more direct control in public policy and governance.

WHEREAS the Royal Commission on Electoral Reform and Party Finance has confirmed public suspicions that there are many inequities in our system of government.

WHEREAS several courts have ruled sections of our electoral law unconstitutional, and the Government has cancelled funding for the program which assisted Canadians to use the courts to challenge unconstitutional rules and practices.

WHEREAS Parliament has chosen not to act to rectify these problems or deal with these exigencies.

WHEREFORE the undersigned, your petitioners, humbly pray and call upon Parliament to enact legislation to allow for a two part referendum on election reform and the first-past-the-post voting system. The first, a choice between our present system and a new one based on proportional representation, and the second to determine which type of proportional representation reform is preferred by Canadians.

AND as in duty bound your Petitioners will ever pray.

DATE _____

PETITION TO:

have Parliament enact legislation to allow for a two part referendum on election reform and the first-past-the-post voting system. The first, a choice between our present system and a new one based on proportional representation, and the second to determine which type of proportional representation reform is preferred by Canadians.

	SIGNATURE	ADDRESS	POSTAL CODE
1.			
2.			
3.			
4.			
5.			
6.			
7.			
8.			
9.			
10.			
11.			
12.			
13.			
14.			
15.			
16.			
17.			
18.			
19.			
20.			
21.			
22			
23.			
24.			
25.			
26.			
27.			
28.			
29.			
30.			

APPENDIX C
REGISTERED POLITICAL PARTIES

ELECTIONS CANADA LIST OF POLITICAL PARTIES

1) REGISTERED

NAME OF PARTY	LEADER	NATIONAL HEADQUARTERS
Christian Heritage Party of Canada	Heather Stillwell	6369 Sundance Drive Surrey, B.C. V3S 8A9 ☎(604) 574-3456 FAX 574-9229
Communist Party of Canada	Miguel Figueroa	290 A Danforth Avenue, Toronto, ON M4K 1N6 ☎(416)469-2446 FAX 469-4063
Confederation of Regions Western Party	Nora Galenzeski	Box 303 Bloomfield, ON K0K 1G0 ☎(613) 476-5365
The Green Party of Canada	Chris Lea	831 Commercial Drive Vancouver, BC V5L 3W6 ☎(604) 254-8165 FAX 254-8166
Liberal Party of Canada	The Honorable Jean Chrétien	200 Laurier Avenue West, Suite 200, Ottawa, ON K1P 6M8 ☎ (613) 237-0740 FAX 235-7208
Libertarian Party of Canada	Hill Cox	1 St. John's Road, Suite 301 Toronto, ON M6P 1T7 ☎ (416) 763-3688 FAX 538-0747
New Democratic Party	The Honorable Audrey McLaughlin	310 Somerset Street West, Ottawa, ON K2P 0J9 ☎(613)236-3613 FAX 230-9950

Parti Rhinocéros	Dominique Langevin	6777 St-Dominique Montréal, QC H2S 3B1 ☎(514) 276-9403 FAX 276-8909
Party for the Commonwealth of Canada	Gilles Gervais	8259 St. Lawrence Blvd. Montréal, QC H2P 2M1 ☎(514)385-5494 FAX 385-9130
Progressive Conservatives	The Right Honorable Kim Campbell	275 Slater Street, 6th floor, Ottawa, ON K1P 5H9 ☎(613)238-6111 FAX 563-7892
Reform Party of Canada	E. Preston Manning	1600-833-4th Avenue S.W., Calgary, AB T2P 0K5 ☎(403)269-1990 FAX 269-4077
Social Credit Party of Canada	Kenneth L. Campbell	Box 100, Milton, ON L9T 2Y3 ☎(416) 878-8461 FAX 878-6600

2) ACCEPTED FOR REGISTRATION

Bloc Québécois	Lucien Bouchard	425 de Maisonneuve Blvd W Room 1475 Montréal, QC H3A 3G5 ☎(514) 499-3000 FAX 499-3638
Canada Party	Joseph. A. Thauberger	1216-12th Avenue East Regina, SK S4N 0M5 ☎(306) 757-0773
Canadian Party for Renewal	Jeffrey Goodman	2733 Lakeshore Blvd., Suite 10, Etobicoke, ON M8V 1H1 ☎(416) 259-4649 FAX 234-8636
Marxist-Leninist Party of Canada	Hardial Singh Bains	171 Dalhousie Street Ottawa, ON K1N 7C7 ☎(613) 235-7052

National Party of Canada	Mel Hurtig	200-250 Portage Avenue, P.O. Box 733 Winnipeg, MB R3C 2L4 ☎(204) 949-2430 FAX 956-2784
Natural Law Party of Canada	Neil Paterson	500 Wilbrod Street Ottawa, ON K1N 6N2 ☎(613) 565-8517 FAX 565-6546
Option Canada Party	Gregory W. Gogan	P.O. Box 252 Pierrefonds, QC H9H 4K9 ☎(514) 624-9026
Parti Nationaliste du Québec	Louis Gravel	19 St-Onge Street, Hull, QC J8Y 5T4 ☎(819) 771-2092
Populist Party for Canada	Benjamin S. Bissett	231-2001 Highway 97 South Kelowna, B.C. V1Z 3E3 ☎(604) 768-4689 FAX 768-4689
Reform of the Monetary Law	Dollard Desjardins	3702 Mousseau Street Montréal, QC H1K 2V5 ☎(514) 354-5818

APPENDIX D

THE MECHANICS OF PARTY CONSTITUTIONS

There are some parts of party constitutions that will be important to organizing for adoption of the Democracy League agenda. An awareness of these will be necessary to the success of the democratic project, because the party establishments are likely to resist our efforts at every opportunity.

The central party apparatus has some controls over riding associations, candidate nominations, and the selection of delegates to a general meeting or leadership convention. The riding associations have considerable autonomy, however, especially those with large memberships, and rules which allow them to resist party executive decisions.

There are many similarities in the constitutions of the various parties. The following analysis provides a summary of the relevant similar sections in the party constitutions with a comparison chart, followed by a description of the relevant sections of each party's constitution and a summary explaining its implications for Democracy League activities. We assume that the political parties and their leaders will find it difficult to denounce us or try to expel us for pursuing a democratic agenda that enjoys broad public support.

GENERAL MEETINGS

All the parties have national conventions, assemblies, or gatherings every two years. It is these meetings which elect the party executive, amend the constitution, review the leader, and decide party policy. The voting delegates at general meetings are primarily elected by the party riding, women's and youth associations.

Proportion of riding delegates at general meetings

PC   associations elect 75 - 85% no minimum

Liberal   associations elect 85% minimum

NDP   associations elect 50 - 85% no minimum

Reform   associations elect 85 - 95% no minimum

CANDIDATE NOMINATION

All parties allow riding associations to nominate candidates but the rules for final approval of candidate nominations are different.

The Canada Election Act requires the Leader or a designated representative of the leader to sign the nomination papers of candidates. Most party constitutions do not specify how the leader will use this authority, but there are examples of the leaders refusing to approve candidates. A recent memorable one was Brian Mulroney's refusal to endorse disgraced cabinet minister Sinclair Stevens when he sought re-election in 1988. Liberal leaders have occasionally rejected candidates but acquired the explicit power to do so at the party's 1992 convention.

Riding Association Selection of Candidate

PC :   association elects

Liberal :   association elects, leader may overrule and appoint

NDP :   association elects, federal council may nullify

Reform :   association elects, executive may nullify

CHANGING PARTY CONSTITUTIONS

All of the parties require different periods of notice for constitutional amendments except the PCs who allow motions from the floor supported with signatures from 100 or more riding associations. The parties have different rules for proposing amendments and all parties except the Reform Party require a two-thirds majority for an amendment to succeed.

PC :   amendment must be presented
                   six weeks in advance

Liberal :   amendment must have been previously
                   adopted by a provincial association, the
                   national executive or a party commission,
                   four weeks notice required

NDP :   amendment must submitted by a riding
                   association or affiliated (voting) group, a
                   provincial party, federal or provincial youth
                   section or chapters, or the party or federal
                   riding council, 60 days notice

Reform :   amendment must be passed by a majority of
                   the members of an association, only a
                   majority vote is needed, 72 days notice, party
                   also allows amendment by referendum

LEADER SELECTION AND REVIEW

Party leaders are elected at leadership conventions and have their leadership confirmed or face review at general conventions or assemblies.

Leadership Confirmation or Review Votes

PC :   first convention after election where party
                doesn't form a government

Liberal :   first convention after every election

NDP :   every assembly (two years)

Reform :   every assembly (two years)

APPEAL PROCESS AND PARTY REFERENDUMS

All parties have an appeal committee, whether the national director, the executive of the party, a special committee struck for the occasion, or some other party body designated as a permanent appeal committee. Only the Reform Party allows member-initiated referendums which can be used as a final appeal.

SUMMARY OF PARTY CONSTITUTIONS

Progressive Conservative Party

Article 3
Constituency associations select candidate and delegates to any meeting.

Article 5
General meetings to be held biannually.

Article 12
Leadership review question only at convention following election where party does not form government.

Article 13
Voting at national meetings, six delegates elected from each constituency association plus three more from its youth organization. Large block of ex-officio or appointed delegates including affiliated organizations, approximately 300 for provincial associations, and a host of others including MPs, Provincial MPPs and MLAs, members of the Senate and other party officials.

Article 17
Appeal to national director by any 10 members of a constituency association and subsequent appeal to steering committee.

Article 18
Amendments to constitution require six weeks notice before meeting, notice suspended if it has supporting signatures of one or more persons from 100 or more recognized constituency associations, two thirds majority required to pass.

Summary

The Progressive Conservative constitution is designed to make it easy to operate within the party. Candidate nominations are seldom overturned by the leader, riding associations control most of the delegates to conventions, and amendments to the constitution are easy to organize although somewhat harder to pass than in the Liberal party. The Democracy League agenda could easily be adopted as party policy through the riding associations to the national convention. The leader is difficult to unseat except when he or she loses an election. It should be noted by those who wanted to get rid of Mulroney so badly over the last few years that it could have been engineered with a little work. If a few thousand people wanting a leadership review had joined the party and taken over enough riding associations to carry a constitutional amendment at a convention, then a review could have been forced in much the same way as Mulroney orchestrated the review that unseated Joe Clark.

Liberal Party

Article 14.(6)
National campaign committee sets rules for each province for candidate nominations. Rule used by Chretien to appoint candidates (from Ontario rules) 3.3 & 3.4 leader may decide a nomination meeting shall not be held and shall designate a candidate.

Article 15
Permanent appeal committee made up of two executive appointments and one from each province, decisions are final.

Article 16
National convention every two years, no more than 15 per cent of delegates can be ex-officio MPs, senators, other candidates, provincial party leaders and association presidents, and others including party executive members. Twelve delegates from each riding, plus riding president, and 4 from youth associations.

Article 17
Leadership review question at first convention after every election.

Article 18
Constitutional amendments, written notice four weeks before date of convention, must have been previously adopted by a provincial association, the national executive, or a party commission, two-thirds majority required.

Summary

The Liberal Party constitution will present some difficulties for the Democracy League. The national campaign committee establishes the nomination rules and the leader has the power to intervene and uses it. The ridings elect the majority of delegates to meetings and leadership conventions of all the parties and this makes it feasible to win the actual vote. These amendments would take longer to organize however, because they must first pass through a provincial association.

New Democratic Party

Article 5
Conventions every two years.

Article 6(3)
Constituency associations get one delegate for 50 members or less, one for each additional fifty members or fraction up to 200, and one for each additional 100 or fraction thereof. NDP has the largest number of additional delegates from affiliated groups, provincial parties, and executive ex-officio appointments.

Article 15
Candidate nominations. The federal council establishes rules including those to achieve affirmative action goals and may intervene and nullify a nomination. Appeal is to the council of the federal party.

Article 16
The constitution may be amended if a resolution is submitted by a riding association or affiliated (voting) group, a provincial party, federal or provincial youth section or chapter, or the party councils. Sixty days notice is required and a two-thirds vote at convention.

Summary

The NDP is the most difficult party to change because nomination rules established by the federal council allow it to nullify a candidacy for many reasons and an appeal goes to the council. Also the federal and provincial wings are combined in a way that will make it difficult for the Democracy League to win a majority of delegates. An amendment to the constitution must be submitted by a riding association or a party organization or council, and would require control of nearly all the riding associations to be passed.

Reform Party

Article 4
Constituency associations have the right to do candidate searches and to recommend potential candidates to executive council of the party. They also nominate candidates but the executive may intervene and nullify nomination of any candidate after consultation and its decision is final.

Article 6
Leadership review at each assembly (convention).

Article 7
An assembly (convention) shall be held every two years.

Article 8
The executive council may initiate a poll or referendum of the party membership. The members may initiate a formal referendum by submitting a petition requesting same containing signatures of 5 per cent of the party membership. In such cases, the vote must be conducted by the executive council within 90 days.

Article 12
The constitution may be amended in response to proposals passed by a majority of the members of a constituency association, or by a party assembly, or by a subcommittee or task force established by the executive council. There must be 72 days notice. At a party assembly, only a majority vote is required to amend. The referendum process in Article 8 may be used to amend as well, provided there is a two thirds majority of the members responding, and a majority vote in a majority of the provinces qualifying for maximum representation on the executive council.

Summary

The Reform Party should be most open to the Democracy League agenda, and we hope its members will use their referendum procedure to make it their party policy.

APPENDIX E
LIBERAL DELEGATE SELECTION PROCEDURE

1990 National Liberal Leadership Convention

Form A-3

Notice of Delegate Election Meeting

NOTICE is hereby given of a Meeting of the _____
Federal Liberal Association, Club or Commission to elect delegates and
alternates to the Liberal Party of Canada Convention.

Date of Meeting: _____
Starting Time: _____
Municipal Address: _____

Those Qualified to Vote
1. a. Residents of the electoral district who are members at
        least _____(___) days prior to the starting time of the Meeting.
    b. Non-residents of the electoral district who were members
        _____(___) days prior to the date of the Meeting.
    c. Residents of the electoral district who are immediate past
        members and who renew their membership prior to the starting time
        of the Meeting.
    d. Non-residents of the electoral district who are immediate
        past members and who renew their membership prior to the
        starting time of the Meeting, so long as they were members or
        immediate past members _____(___) months prior to the
        date of the Meeting.

2. Provided that all such individuals referred to in Paragraph 1 are:
    a. Fourteen (14) years of age and over
    b. Ordinarily resident in Canada
    c. Not a member of any other federal political party within
        Canada
    d. Not a member of another Federal Constituency Association

Other Information
1. Annual membership dues: $_____
2. Maximum non-resident members: _____ % of total
    membership.
3. A member must sign his or her own membership application
    and pay their own prescribed membership fee as provided for
    by the provincial or territorial association Constitution and the
    Constitution of said federal Constituency Association.
4. A "CUT-OFF" Meeting will take place or has taken place
    at_____ o'clock p.m. on _____ day 199___, to determine
    those eligible to vote or renew at the Meeting.

For Further Information Contact
President: _____   Secretary: _____
Address: _____   Address: _____
Phone: _____   Phone: _____
Date of Notice: _____

Form A-5

Application for Membership

To: _____
Indicate name of:

- federal Constituency Association
- student club
- women's club

I hereby apply to join the association or club named above, and I certify that I am

- 14 years or over
- ordinarily resident of Canada
- not a member of any other federal political party within Canada
- not a member of any other federal Constituency Association*

_____
(Signature)

_____
(Date)

Applicant's Name: _____

Home Address: _____
 (Street)   (City)

_____
 (Province/Territory)   (Postal Code)

Mailing Address (if different than above): _____

Phone Nos: _____ (B) _____ (R)

Date of Birth: _____
 (Youth Membership)

Fill in if applicable: I am currently a member of _____
federal Constituency Association. Effective immediately, I hereby resign my membership in that association and I undertake to so advise that association.

_____
(Signature)

Note: (All associations are advised to include on application forms other requirements specified in their respective constitutions.)

1990 National Liberal Leadership Convention

SCHEDULE A

SCRIPT FOR THE CHAIR OF A
DELEGATE SELECTION MEETING

(Do not read out portions in brackets)

1. Ladies and Gentlemen, my name is _____ **and I call to ORDER the** (name of Federal Constituency Association, Club or Commission) **Delegate Selection Meeting. Membership renewals and payment of membership fees are now closed. Anyone eligible to renew and in line to do so may still renew.**

2. I am pleased to be here this evening and congratulate you on the organization of your Meeting. I bring greetings from the President (of the Provincial or Territorial Association) _____ _____ **and the rest of the table officers.**

3. Those members who are eligible to vote at tonight's Meeting are on a list which is in the possession of the Returning Officer. Those members who have renewed their membership this evening are being added to the list now. The eligibility of members to vote or renew their membership was determined at the CUT-OFF by (the Provincial or Territorial Association) **official held prior to this evening's Meeting in accordance with** (the Provincial or Territorial Association) **Constitution.**

(Read the rules governing the nomination and election of delegates as follows)

4. (For Constituency Association, Club or Commission) **The Rules of procedure for the election of your delegates and alternates are:**

> **a) In order to be nominated the person must be a member in good standing of the Constituency Association, Club or Commission, and must either be present or have submitted written consent to stand for the position.**
>
> **b) Each nominator shall give only his/her name and may speak in support of the nominee for** _____( ) **minute(s).**
>
> **c) The seconder shall give his/her name and shall speak no**

225

further.

d) **Nominees will be called in reverse order of nomination and may speak for _____.(·) minute(s).**

e) **If a nominee wishes to withdraw, he/she must do so without speaking in favour of any other nominee.**

f) **I have appointed _____ as Returning Officer.**

g) **Each nominee may appoint one (1) scrutineer for each Deputy Returning Officer.**

h) **One ballot shall be issued for all positions. We are required to elect 12 delegates, four of whom shall be men, four of whom shall be women, and four of whom shall be youth (two of whom shall be men and two of whom shall be women). Youth members shall not be restricted only to those delegate or alternate positions set aside for youth. Therefore, the four youth nominees receiving the highest votes and also meeting the gender qualifications shall be the youth delegates. Respecting the gender qualifications of the remaining delegate positions, the nominees receiving the next highest votes regardless of age, shall be the remaining delegates.**
(Meeting Chairs are referred to Interpretation Bulletin # 2 for further clarification)

i) **In order to be a youth delegate or alternate, a member must not celebrate his/her 26th birthday prior to June 19, 1990 which is the date of the opening of registration.**

j) **The Chair shall announce the names of the successful candidates. Otherwise, the result of the voting and the number of votes cast for each candidate shall not be disclosed.**

5. I will now call for nominations for the position of delegate to the 1990 National Leadership Convention.

(An official shall list the names of nominees and whether they are women, eligible youth or men on a blackboard or flip chart as they are nominated. Appoint a person to list the names before you take the Chair.)

(After each nomination is seconded, ask for further nominations. When there is no response to the call for further nominations, declare nominations are closed.)

I declare that nominations are closed.

I will now call upon each nominee to speak.

(Call upon nominees in reverse order of nomination)

6. The following are instructions for balloting:

> **a) A single ballot shall be issued to each member entitled to vote;**
> **b) No proxy ballots are allowed; and**
> **c) A ballot will not be invalidated provided that, in the opinion of the Returning Officer, the nominee can be identified with reasonable certainty.**

Is everything clear?

Scrutineers for the nominees please report to the Returning Officer.

Please proceed to (balloting location) **to receive, mark and cast your ballot.**

(All ballots must be initialed, prior to voting, by the Chair and/or the Returning Officer.)

(The Chair will ask if there is anyone who wishes to vote who has not yet done so. Then declare balloting is closed.)

Balloting is now closed.

(When results are available, they shall be relayed to the Chair.)

(The Chair will deliver to the General Secretary of the Convention in the envelope provided, the list of delegates and alternates, with the addresses and phone numbers on the prescribed forms. If there has been a vote, ballots, voting records and priority alternate forms shall be returned to the Provincial or Territorial Association, where ballots will be destroyed after the appeal period has expired.)

7. Ladies and Gentlemen, I now have the results of the ballot.

The male delegates including the two (2) male youth are:
(read the names of the male delegates.)

The female delegates including the two (2) female youth are:
(read the names of the female delegates)

The male alternate is:
(read the name of the male alternate.)

The female alternate is:
(read the name of the female alternate.)

The male youth alternate is:
(read the name of the male youth alternate.)

The female youth alternate is:
(read the name of the female youth alternate.)

8. Ballots must be retained by the Provincial or Territorial Association until all levels of Appeal have been exhausted. I have instructed the Returning Officer to transfer the ballots to the Provincial or Territorial Association.

APPENDIX F
MODEL PROGRESSIVE
CONSERVATIVE CONSTITUTION

Article 1. Name

1. The name of the Association shall be "The Progressive
    Conservative Association of_____"
    herein referred to as the Association.

Article 2. Purpose, Aims and Principles

2.1 To promote the principles and policies of the Progressive
     Conservative Party of Canada.

2.2 To call a convention for the nomination of the Progressive
     Conservative Candidate for each federal election.

2.3 To elect and re-elect a Progressive Conservative Member
     to the House of Commons using all proper means to do so.

2.4 To secure, maintain and adequately fund a thorough
     organization of the Progressive Conservative Party
     throughout the constituency.

2.5 To establish a plan and execute a program of public
     involvement with an aim to enhance the visibility
     and good standing of the Association and the Progressive
     Conservative Member of Parliament.

2.6 As a further matter of principle, the Association commits
     itself to strive to ensure the equality of men and women
     and to reflect the demographic composition of the
     constituency.

2.7 To select delegates and alternates to meetings and
     conventions of or called by the Progressive Conservative
     Association of Canada.

Article 3. **Membership**

3.1 The Membership of the Association shall be composed of every person who complies with each of the following:

3.1.1 is a citizen or permanent resident of Canada;

3.1.2 maintains his or her principal residence within the constituency or is a member of the constituency association executive;

3.1.3 actively supports the aims and principles of the Party;

3.1.5 has attained the age of 14; and

3.1.6 has paid the membership fee prescribed by the Association's executive.

Article 4. **Voting**

4.1 All members shall be entitled to vote on;

4.1.1 the selection of delegates and alternates to any national meeting; and

4.1.2 the selection of any Progressive Conservative Candidate for elections to the House of Commons;

4.1.3 the selection of the executive of the constituency association;

4.1.4 any other matter upon which a vote is required.

Article 5. **Executive**

5.1 The Executive shall consist of elected officers and certain ex-officio members.

5.1.1 The Officers to be elected shall be; President, Vice-President, Second Vice-President, Secretary, Treasurer and at least ten (10) Directors.

5.1.2 The ex-officio members shall be; Progressive Conservative Member of Parliament and or the most recently nominated candidate; the Association's immediate Past President; the constituency's Women's Association President, and the constituency's Youth Association President.

Article 6. **Election of the Executives**

6.1 Officers of the Executive shall be elected at the Annual Meeting of the Association and shall hold office until the next Annual Meeting.

6.2 Wherever possible, officers of the executive shall reflect all significant constituency demographics.

6.3 Any executive officer who is absent, without reasonable excuse, from three consecutive executive meetings and/or is unable or unwilling to continue holding office shall cease to be an officer of the executive. A replacement at the executive's discretion, may be appointed.

Article 7. **Duties of the Executive**

7.1 The Executive shall strive to meet the purposes, aims and principles of the Association pursuant to Article 2;

7.2 The Executive shall establish committees they deem as necessary in addition to the following committees;

7.2.1 A nominating committee to seek out and propose a list of supporters to stand for election as officers at the Annual Meeting of the Association. This committee shall be chaired by the immediate Past President of the Association or in his/her absence or incapacity, a Past-President of the Association appointed by the

Executive. Inclusive of Chairperson the Committee shall number five individuals of whom no more than two current officers may serve as members. At least two members of the committee shall be Association members who are not members of the Association Executive.

7.2.2 A Fundraising Committee to establish a plan and execute means of raising funds for the Association. This committee will report to the Association's Executive.

7.2.3 A Planning and Priorities Committee to establish a plan of action in respect to Association events and functions. This Committee will report to the Association's Executive.

7.3 Except where expressly limited the Executive shall:

7.3.1 pass by-laws respecting the organization and good management of the Association. By-laws passed are subject to ratification by members of the Association at a General Meeting.

7.3.2 have all power and authority which might be exercised by the Association at a General Meeting.

7.4 The required quorum for an Executive Meeting shall be six Members of the Executive.

7.5 The duties of the individual officers of the Executive shall be:

7.5.1 **The President**

The president shall be the Chief Executive Officer of the Association and shall supervise and have the responsibility for the management of the affairs and business of the Association and he or she shall preside at all meetings of the Association and shall be an ex-officio member of all committees of the Association. The President shall be responsible for the vigorous promotion by the Association of the purposes, aims and principles of this Constitution. The President shall call meetings of the Executive when deemed necessary or at the written request of not less than six members of the Executive. In any event, there shall be at least two executive meetings held in each calendar year. The President shall give such reasonable notice of any Executive meeting as the circumstances permit with 48 hours being the minimum.

7.5.2 **First and Second Vice-President**

The First and Second Vice-Presidents shall carry out duties as may be assigned to them by the Executive or the President, and the Vice-Presidents in order of seniority shall preside at meetings of the Executive and of the Association, in the absence of the President.

7.5.3 **Secretary**

The Secretary shall keep minutes of all meetings of the Association and shall conduct all ordinary correspondence. The Secretary shall be charged with the responsibilities of giving notice of all meetings to the Executive and to the members of the Association in accordance with this Constitution.

7.5.4 **Treasurer**

The Treasurer shall receive all monies which are the property of the Association and shall keep an accurate record thereof and shall submit the Association's accounts annually, or more often if required by the Association of the Executive, for an audit.

7.5.5 **Directors**

The Directors shall perform such duties as assigned to them by the Executive. Areas of responsibility include Membership; Communications, Special Events, Poll Organization and Multiculturalism.

Article 8.   **Fees**

8.1   Membership fees shall be set by the Executive annually.

Article 9. **Annual, General and Special Meeting**

9.1   The Annual Meeting of the Association shall be held during the month of_____and at place and time determined by the association Executive.

9.2   Adequate public notice for an Annual, General or Special meeting shall be given by a mailing to all members of record at least thirty (30) days, but no more than forty-five (45) days, in advance of the meeting.

   9.2.1 In addition, advertisements must be published at least two (2) weeks in advance of the meeting in a newspaper or newspapers having general circulation in the constituency.

9.3   The required quorum for a Annual, General or Special Meeting shall be twenty (20) members.

9.4   A majority of the members voting at any Annual, General or Special Meeting shall be conclusive.

   9.4.1 In the case of a vote to reconsider or over-rule a decision of the chair, a two-thirds majority shall be required.

   9.4.2 In the case of a tie-vote, the presiding Chairman shall cast the deciding vote, being the only occasion on which the Chairman is entitled to vote.

9.5   At every Annual Meeting of the Association at least one auditor shall be appointed by the Association for the audit of the accounts of the treasurer, such auditor however shall not be a member of the Executive.

9.6   The order of business at an Annual, General or Special Meeting shall be:

   A.   Minutes of previous meeting

B. Reports of committees (Annual Meeting only)

C. Correspondence

D. Treasurer's Report (Annual Meeting only)

E. Auditor's Report and appointment of auditor for ensuing year (Annual Meeting only)

F. Election of Officers (Annual Meeting only)

G. Other Business

H. Adjournment

9.7 No membership shall be issued during the two weeks prior to an Annual, General or Special Meeting, except for the renewal of memberships which were valid for the last meeting of the Association.

Article 10. **Right to Appeal**

10.1 Any (10) Party supporters may assert in writing to the national director that the requirements of Article 3 of the Progressive Conservative Association of Canada Constitution are not being met by the executive of the Association.

10.2 When such appeal is received, the national director shall pursue the course of action as stated in Article 16 of the Progressive Conservative Association of Canada Constitution.

Article 11. **Delegate and Candidate Selection Process**

11.1 Delegates and Candidates shall be selected in accordance with the governing provisions of the constitution of the Progressive Conservative Association of Canada.

Article 12. **Candidate Nomination Meeting Procedure**

12.1 The Executive shall call a meeting as required to select by secret ballot a Progressive Conservative candidate for each Federal Election.

12.2 Notice of such meeting shall be given to all members either by mail or by publication of a notice, in a newspaper or newspaper having general circulation in the constituency at least two weeks prior to the date of such meeting.

12.3 No membership shall be issued during the two weeks prior to a meeting called for the purposes of selecting a Progressive Conservative candidate, except for the renewal of memberships which were valid for the last meeting of the Association.

12.4 The proceedings at a Nomination Meeting shall take place as follows:

A. Calling the meeting to order.

B. Reading the notice to call the convention.

C. Calling for nomination:

i) each nomination must be moved and seconded by voting members in writing

ii) each nominee must consent to the nomination in writing and pledge support in writing to the successful nominee.

D. Declaring nominations closed and the appointing of the returning officer and one scrutineer by the Chairman and one scrutineer by each candidate for each ballot box which is to be used by connection with the taking of the vote.

E. Any nominee shall have the privilege of withdrawing before the vote is taken or at any time during the balloting.

F.	Addresses by nominees shall be in alphabetical order and the duration of the speeches shall be determined by the Chairman.

G.	Voting by secret ballot.

H.	An absolute majority shall be necessary for the election. If no nominee has an absolute majority after the first ballot, further balloting shall be conducted until an absolute majority has been obtained by one nominee. On each ballot, subsequent to the first, the nominee having the lowest number of votes shall drop out and only the remaining nominees shall be voted upon.

I.	After completion of the balloting, the Chairman shall declare the election of a Candidate and shall invite the Candidate to address the Convention.

Article 13. **Amendments**

13.	Amendments to this Constitution may be made at any general meeting of the association providing that written notice of the proposed amendment shall have been given to the Secretary of the Association at least five (5) weeks prior to the meeting at which it will be proposed. The Secretary shall include notice that an amendment or amendments have been proposed in the notice calling such meeting.

DEMOCRACY, EH?

ETOBICOKE-LAKESHORE FEDERAL PROGRESSIVE CONSERVATIVE ASSOCIATION

One Evans Avenue, Etobicoke, Ontario M8Z 1H4   (416) 255-9289

1993 MEMBERSHIP APPLICATION

NAME: _____

ADDRESS: _____

_____

POSTAL CODE: _____

PHONE #: _____ (RES) _____ (BUS)

TYPE OF MEMBERSHIP

SINGLE   ($10.00)   _____

YOUTH*   ($ 5.00)   _____ (14 yrs to 30 yrs)

SENIOR*   ($ 5.00)   _____ (65 yrs and over)

SUSTAINING ($20.00 & over) _____ (a tax receipt will be issued)

* proof of age may be requested for certain types of membership.

● PLEASE RETURN THIS FORM WITH YOUR MEMBERSHIP FEE TO:

One Evans Avenue
Etobicoke, Ontario
M8Z 1H4

● PLEASE MAKE ALL CHEQUES PAYABLE TO:

Etobicoke Lakeshore Federal Progressive
Conservative Association

238

Index

INDEX

Lambert, Marcel, 65
Lange, David, 78
LaRouche, Lyndon, 110
Laurier, Sir Wilfrid, 29, 37, 114-115
Laxer, James, 193
Lea, Chris, 62, 154-155
Leaders' debates, 154-155, 158, 163, 167-170, 177-178
Leadership financing, 54, 148
LeBreton, Marjory, 150
LeDuc, Lawrence, 28
Levesque Rene, 39, 85
Lewis, Bob, 150
Liberal Party, 29-33, 35-42, 47, 50, 53, 58-59, 65, 67, 85, 93, 107-108, 117, 146-148, 155, 157-159, 169-170, 190, 193-194, 201
Liberal-Social Democratic Alliance, 77
Liberals for Life, 193-194,
Libertarian Party, 35, 94, 159
Lieutenant Governor, 128
Lobbyists, 141-142
Lombard League, 82
Lortie, Pierre, 48-51, 153
Lougheed, Peter, 39
Lowenstein, Daniel, 129

M
Macdonald, Donald, 86-87
Macdonald, Sir John A., 29
Macdonald Royal Commission, 86-87, 92
Mackie, T., 38
Mackenzie, Robert, 190
Maclean's-Decima poll, 102
Manitoba, 117, 127-128
Manning, Ernest, 85
Manning, Preston, 154-155, 166, 189
Marin, Charles-Eugene, 62

Martin, Paul, 194
Massachussetts, 111
McCash, Dan, 193
McKenna, Frank, 39
McLaughlin, Audrey, 154-155
McQueen, Trina, 185
Meighen, Arthur, 123
Mercredi, Ovide, 76
Mill, John Stuart, 73, 98
Miller, Frank, 177
Mills, Dennis, 138, 143-144
Milliken, Peter, 62
Minority rights, 131
Moniere, D., 169
Mulroney, Brian, 19-21, 23, 34, 42-43, 48-51, 54, 73, 86, 101, 106-108, 136, 140, 150, 176, 190, 193, 199
Murphy, Don, 179
Murphy, Rod, 62

N
Nader, Ralph, 111, 200
National Action Committee on the Status of Women (NAC), 198, 199
National Citizens' Coalition (NCC), 55-57, 178-180, 199
National Election Studies, 32
National Party, 35, 37, 44, 58, 63, 77-78, 94, 154, 158, 167-168, 188
Negative voting, 43-44
Netherlands, 89, 91
New Democratic Party (NDP), 21, 32-33, 35-42, 44, 50, 53, 58, 66, 80, 92-94, 97, 107-108, 119, 146-148, 157-159, 167, 190, 196-198
New Zealand, 43, 88, 91, 134
New Zealand Electoral Reform Commission, 87
New Zealand referendum, 77
Newfoundland, 118

42, 76, 79-80, 116, 177
Turner, John, 30, 107, 108, 150, 176, 194

U
Union Nationale, 85
United Kingdom, 77, 109, 136, 161, 164, 175
United States of America (USA), 109-112, 125, 128, 161, 163, 200
U.S. Supreme Court, 129

V
Vander Zalm, Bill, 120
Vezina, Greg, 26, 50, 167-170, 172, 186, 200
Vickers and Benson Advertising, 179
Vote of confidence, 135

W
Wappel, Tom, 193-194
Washington, 110
Western Canada Wilderness Society, 200
White, Bob, 196
Wilson, Geoff, 62
Wilson, Gordon, 170
Wilson, Martha, 185
Winters, Robert, 30

X

Y

Z